Beanie Babies
COLLECTOR'S GUIDE

HOLLY STOWE

This publication is not authorized or licensed by Ty, Inc.
Publications International, Ltd., is not affiliated with Ty, Inc.

PUBLICATIONS INTERNATIONAL, LTD.

Holly Stowe is an avid Beanie Babies collector and writer. Her Beanie Babies articles have appeared in publications such as *Beanie Collector* and *Beanie Mania*, as well as on the Internet.

All photography by Brian Warling/Brian Warling Photography. Photo styling by Lisa Wright.

ACKNOWLEDGMENTS:

Special thanks to the generous collectors who loaned their Beanie Babies collections for this book: Lindsay Gehrls; Kelley Hardman; Cheryl Damato; Frank Magos; Diana Petersen and her generous customer, Judy, with Diana Petersen Collectibles at 1452 Miner Street, Des Plaines, IL 60016, 847/296-6335; Marianna and Dominic Stocco; Rachel Kagan; Leah Benjamin; and Jan Schroeder.

Contents

The Beanie Explosion

The craze over Beanie Babies is about as far-reaching as any you'll ever see. People from all walks of life collect Beanies. Some collect to make money on the secondary market, some as an investment, and some simply for the love of these little "babies." Whatever your reason for collecting, rest assured, you are not alone.

THE HISTORY OF TY, INC.

So how did this all get started?

In 1962, H. Ty Warner, a recent graduate of Kalamazoo College, went to work for Dakin, Inc., a well-known manufacturer of stuffed animals. Warner worked for Dakin for 18 years. In 1986, he settled in the western suburbs of Chicago, near Oakbrook, where he started Ty, Inc., setting out to do what he had done for years with Dakin: produce stuffed animals.

Warner's first designs were four plush Himalayan cats (Smokey, Angel, Peaches, and Ginger), which have become highly valued. The cats and other plush animals were followed in 1991 by a series of annual collectible bears. Ty's plush line has continued to grow in popularity—especially with the help of the Beanie Babies craze. Collectors unable to find Beanies in stores often turned to other Ty lines, such as Pillow Pals, Attic Treasures, and Country Cousins. Many people have predicted that the plush line is likely to become as popular as Beanie Babies.

BEANIE BABIES ARE BORN

With his line of plush toys costing $10 to $20, Warner came up with a design and marketing strategy for a child-sized toy that would be similar to the plush line but within a child-sized budget. Thus, the original nine Beanie Babies—

Original nine Beanie Babies

Spot the dog (spotless), Squealer the pig, Patti the platypus, Pinchers (Punchers) the lobster, Chocolate the moose, Flash the dolphin, Splash the whale, Cubbie (Brownie) the bear, and Legs the frog—were presented at a toy convention in late 1993. They were introduced to the world in January 1994. Six months later, 25 new Beanies made their appearance.

The marketing strategy? The basis of all economics: supply and demand. To limit availability (supply), and keep the product flow and prices somewhat regulated, Ty, Inc., chose to distribute Beanie Babies through a network of specialty stores rather than larger chains. To create demand, Ty worked out a schedule of "planned obsolescence." A certain number of times each year, some Beanies would be retired while new ones were issued.

As with most things, the frenzy didn't happen overnight, nor was the entire country taken by storm. The eye of the storm was, naturally, the Chicago area, Ty, Inc.'s home turf. But it took two years or more for the storm to really develop even there. By the latter part of 1996, the storm was a full-blown tornado with gusts reaching out to other areas of the country.

TEENIE BEANIES

Then...April 11, 1997. McDonald's started a new Happy Meal promotion, issuing Teenie Beanies for ten Beanie Babies. The set included Teenie Chocolate, Chops, Goldie, Lizz, Patti, Pinky, Quacks, Seamore, Snort, and Speedy. Planned as a five-week promotion with two Teenie Beanies to be featured each week, McDonald's was forced to call a halt after only ten days because all five weeks' worth of Teenies were gone. Some stores sold out completely in the first weekend! All this in spite of the fact that McDonald's, realizing they had underestimated demand, did very little advertising for the promotion.

Keeping this in mind, McDonald's announced a second Happy Meal Teenie Beanie promotion slated to begin May 22, 1998, and featuring Teenie Doby, Bongo, Twigs, Inch, Pinchers, Happy, Mel, Scoop, Bones, Zip, Waddle, and Peanut. In preparation, McDonald's ordered twice the production of each Teenie Beanie, but to no avail. Once again, the Teenies sold out in most McDonald's stores by the end of the first weekend.

Teenie Beanies first set

Teenie Beanies second set

Rumors have already begun of a third Teenie Beanie promotion in 1999, but one has to wonder just how many Teenies will have to be made in order to keep up with the demand.

BEANIES ONLINE

The Internet has played no small part in the Beanie Babies craze. In August 1996, Ty opened its own website (http://www.ty.com) to promote its entire line of toys, but the focus of the site was, of course, on Beanie Babies. Since January 1, 1997, announcements of retired and new Beanies have been made via the website. According to Ty's own count, over 1.5 billion people have been served. Given the difficulty of even reaching the site during peak times, one wonders what the count of "hits" would be if everyone could reach the site every time they tried!

A number of other sites exist to provide the latest news, information, and gossip on Beanies. A site called Beaniemom's Net Letter contains a weekly updated pricing guide on retired pieces; nationwide swap meet and trade listings that are updated almost daily; and information on important news items such as counterfeits, promotions, and fund raisers. Like many websites, Beaniemom is done purely for the love of Beanies and not as a capital venture. Many online auctions and trading boards exist as well, but be careful trading online. Make sure you get references and read the many helpful hints about Beanie transactions on the Internet.

> ### 5 BEANIE WEBSITES
>
> 1. Ty, Inc.: http://www.ty.com
> 2. Beaniemom's Net Letter: http://www.beaniemom.com
> 3. The Beanie Philes: http://www.beaniephiles.com
> 4. Ctoys.com: http://www.ctoys.com/news/
> 5. eBay Auctions: http://www.ebay.com/

The Internet has been a driving force in the prices of Beanies—especially retired Beanies, but also currents and hard-to-finds. Ty has long been concerned about pricing and the secondary market, and the company has recently taken steps to try to keep retail prices down and to attempt to slow, if not stop, the sale of Beanies by retailers to secondary dealers. Legally, Ty cannot set a maximum price for Beanie retailers, however, the company can—and did—send a letter out in April 1998, indicating its expectations of retailers and stating that retailers who were found to be in violation of Ty's policies could lose their accounts. Ty's stand underlines the company's commitment to keeping Beanies primarily as a children's toy.

THE GRAY MARKET

Ty has also worked to keep Beanies intended for a given market within that market. Maple and Britannia, for example, are meant to be sold exclusively in Canada and the United Kingdom, respectively. When these Beanies are brought into the United States for resale, what is known as a "gray market" is created. Ty has involved U.S. Customs in trying to stem the tide of these gray-market Beanies. Customs officials have taken action by seizing shipments of Beanies, requisitioning hand-carried Beanies, and, in some cases, requiring that the Beanie tags be cut or the Beanies be returned to their point of sale. At this time, the overall effect of these measures is unknown, but the primary result seems to have been merely to increase the prices of the gray-market Beanies.

DETERMINING VALUE

Beanie prices are based on a Beanie that is in mint condition with mint tags. The Beanie's tags, especially its hang tags, are actually worth about 40–50 percent of the Beanie's value, though the tag more greatly affects the value of the recently retired Beanies than it does that of the older retireds. Many of the older Beanies were retired long before the frenzy began, and people didn't concern themselves with the condition of the tag. The oldest Beanies are rare enough that many devoted collectors are happy to have one with or without a tag. More-recent retireds, especially those from October 1997 and later, are easily found in mint condition with mint tags. Even a slight crease or bend can devalue a Beanie anywhere from 10 to 40 percent. A heavily creased or mangled hang tag may be considered to have about the same value as no tag at all.

There are currently five generations of hang (also called "swing") tags. These are the heart-shaped tags attached to the Beanie's ear with a plastic connector. The older the generation of hang tag, the more valuable the Beanie. There is no hard-and-fast rule about just how much an older hang tag adds to the Beanie's value, but, as a general guideline, first-generation hang tags currently add $300 to $350 to the going price of *the most recent version of the Beanie.* Second-generation tags add $200 to $250; third-generation tags add $100 to $150; and fourth-generation tags add perhaps $10. Redesigned Beanies are an exception to this rule: The earlier versions are usually more valuable than the most recent.

Another exception belongs to Beanies who have been redesigned and released with the same hang tag found on the previous version. For example, take the tie-dyed version of Lizzy the lizard. Tie-dyed Lizzy came with a third-generation hang tag but was redesigned as the blue/black Lizzy. This version also came with a third-generation hang tag. A third-generation blue/black Lizzy runs between $120 and $180 at this writing, with an additional $20 to $30 tacked on for her most recent version, as well as $100 to $150 for the third-generation tag. But what about tie-dyed Lizzy, worth between $900 and $1,100 with mint tags? A third-generation tag from a blue/black Lizzy could increase the value of tie-dyed Lizzy significantly.

Which, of course, brings us to the ethics of "retagging" Beanies. Technically, once a Beanie has been altered in any way from the way it left the factory, it's not considered to be in truly mint condition. That includes even removing the tag and the connector from the Beanie's ear and replacing it intact later. Beanies should be retagged only with the tags with which they were originally released, and when a Beanie is sold, any retagging should be disclosed to the potential buyer.

To protect yourself on the secondary market, make sure you know which Beanies came with which tags, and make sure the tush tag matches the hang tag as well. Unfortunately, some unethical people will do whatever it takes to make a buck—including faking a "more valuable" tag.

Collectors should also note that while there was a time when Beanies with the wrong tags were uncommon, those days are over. Mistags, even tush tags with the wrong names, are fairly common. Over 1,400 different mistags had been noticed at last count. A few mistags—those that affect an entire production run—are considered "classic," but don't get caught up in paying extra for a Beanie just because it doesn't have its own tag. Remember that hang tags are easily switched and not necessarily a factory error to begin with.

> **CLASSIC MISTAGS**
> Quacker instead of Quackers
> Spook instead of Spooky
> Tuck instead of Tusk
> Sparky with a Dotty tush tag
> Echo and Waves with each others' hang and tush tags
> Iggy and Rainbow with each others' hang and tush tags (or is it really each others' plush?)

HANG TAGS

There are five generations of hang tags. Chances are you may have seen only the fourth- or fifth-generation hang tags. All generations of the hang tag are heart shaped; they are primarily red with gold foil edging; and all have the name "Ty" on the front in white.

First-Generation Hang Tags

This is the tag that was on the original nine Beanies as well as a few others that came out early in Beanie history. The heart shape is a little shorter from top to bottom than on the later tags, and the hole for the connector is at the side of the tag rather than in the upper corner. This tag is not folded over like the other generations. The "ty" lettering on the front is skinny, and the yellow star found on fourth- and fifth-generation tags has not yet appeared. The back of the tag features the Beanie name and style number as well as the company information.

Second-Generation Hang Tags

The second-generation hang tag shares its proportions with the first-generation tag. The "ty" on the front is still skinny, but now the hole for the connector is in the upper left corner

of the heart, and the tag is folded over like a book cover. The company information has been moved to the inside left.

The inside right of the tag acts as a gift tag, with the words "to," "from," and "with love." The back of the tag says "retain tag for reference." This style tag was in use until early- to mid-1995.

Third-Generation Hang Tags

This tag was referred to as "old tag" until recently, because by the time the majority of Beanie collectors jumped on the boat, fourth-generation tags were already in use. Many of these collectors didn't even realize there were two incarnations of tags before the third-generation tag!

This tag was used from mid-1995 to mid-1996. The heart is slightly more square, and the "ty" lettering on the front has fattened up and is now referred to as the "bubble ty." The insides and back of the tag haven't changed significantly.

Fourth-Generation Hang Tags

The most widely found of the extinct hang tags is the fourth-generation tag, introduced in mid-1996 with the Righty, Lefty, Libearty, and Maple releases. (These four Beanies were among the summer 1996 releases that never had third-generation tags.) Many changes were found on the

fourth-generation tags, starting with the appearance of a yellow star on the front. Within the star are the words "BEANIE ORIGINAL BABY." The "ty" on the front is no longer edged in gold. The inside left of the tag still contains the company information, but the right side

is very different. Each Beanie now has a birthday and, instead of the "to/from" area, a poem telling a little bit about the Beanie's personality. On the bottom of the inside right, Ty invites people to visit their website.

Fifth-Generation Hang Tags

The fifth-generation hang tag came at the same time as the release of the January 1998 "newbeans." At first glance, the tag is almost identical to the fourth-generation tag. The primary difference between the two is a change in the typeface used. The style number has been dropped from the inside (though it still appears in the bar code on the back of the tag), and the Beanie's birthday is now spelled out rather than in numeric form. "The Beanie Babies Collection" has a registered mark, and the website information has been shortened.

Another thing to look for on the fifth-generation hang tag is a typographical error within the yellow star. Some styles are misspelled "ORIGIINAL." A number of Beanies have been reported to have this error, most notably Floppity, Hippity, Hoppity, Valentino, Curly, Peace, Blackie, Squealer, and Roary.

Tush Tags

If only the tush tags were as easy to differentiate between as the hang tags are! Fortunately, some of the changes in tush tags have been minor and are not considered a separate and distinct generation. The very first tush tags to appear were black and white with four lines of lettering. The lettering ran the long way on the tush tag rather than across it, as it does on the red-and-white tush tags. There was no Ty heart. All the four-line, black-and-white tush tags feature 1993 copyright dates. These appear only on "pre-Beanie Beanies" like the deep-fuchsia Patti, Punchers, and Brownie.

First-Generation Tush Tags

Still in black and white and in use until midway through the third-generation hang tags, the first-generation tush tag has five lines of printing and either a 1993 or 1995 copyright date. The name "Beanie Babies" doesn't appear on the tag.

Second-Generation Tush Tags

Late in 1995 or early in 1996, Ty changed the tush tag dramatically. Now white with red ink, the tush tag bears the Ty heart on one side (still no mention of the name "Beanie Babies") and consumer information and copyright date on the other. (It's interesting to note that Beanies with a "recycled" style number keep the copyright date of their predecessor.)

Third-Generation Tush Tags

The next incarnation of tush tag was born when the fourth-generation hang tags came along in mid-1996. The words "The Beanie Baby Collection," with a ™ to indicate trademark, are found above the Ty heart on the red-and-white tag, and, below the heart, the Beanie's name appears. The tag itself and the printing are smaller than the previous generation. In mid-1997, clear stickers started appearing over the Ty hearts, bearing a small red star in the upper left corner. These stickers were a transition into the fourth-generation tush tags.

Fourth-Generation Tush Tags

Essentially the same as the third-generation tag, the fourth generation features a small red star printed above and to the left of the Ty heart. This tush tag began appearing in early fall 1997.

Fifth-Generation Tush Tags

Still essentially the same tag as its predecessor, the fifth-generation tush tag began appearing in late fall 1997. The Beanie's name now shows a small ™, and there is also a registered mark after the words "Beanie Babies" in "The Beanie Babies Collection."

Sixth-Generation Tush Tags

Around the time fifth-generation hang tags appeared, sixth-generation tush tags came out. The only difference is that now the entire phrase "The Beanie Babies Collection" is registered. Many collectors consider the differences among the fourth- through sixth-generation tush tags so slight that they could easily be considered one generation. Expect to see another tush tag change in mid- to late-1998.

PROTECTING YOURSELF AGAINST COUNTERFEITS

Counterfeit Beanies have become more and more of a problem over time. One of the ways to protect yourself from unknowingly spending money on counterfeits is to really study the tags. And, as mentioned previously, make sure you know what year your Beanie was copyrighted. Another good idea is to try to find one that you're sure is the real thing (such as at a Ty retailer), and compare. For people with access to the Internet, the Beaniemom website maintains a page devoted to counterfeit Beanies and a list of potential traits of various counterfeits. If in doubt, remember the old saying: If it sounds too good to be true, it probably is. Buyers should always try to buy from Ty retailers or from someone with good references.

USING THIS GUIDE

What goes into determining whether a Beanie is a good investment or a highly recommended one? For the serious Beanie collector, it's obvious that every older retired (prior to January 1, 1997) is highly recommended, but the current prices on these Beanies make them out of reach for most people. Unless you are driven to have every Beanie, your best bet is to look at more-recent retireds. The vast majority will never obtain the level of the older retireds simply because there are more of them available as collectors have been taking better care of them, but these are the Beanies that are more within the reach of the average collector.

So, instead of aiming for the older and rarer Beanies, focus on spreading out your investment with Beanies that may not even be retired yet but have a bright future. These include any of the Beanie bears, which are by far the most popular Beanie group, as well as any of the Beanies that have Teenie Beanie counterparts. More-recently retired Beanies are also recommended, but don't rush to buy one just after it retires. The trend in prices has been a significant increase just after a retirement, followed by a drop (or "correction") about six weeks after an announcement. Thus, six weeks after a retirement announcement is a great time to buy. Prices generally stay lower until the next retirement.

This guide lists currents, even hard-to-find currents, at the going retail price of $5–$7. You don't need to be the first on your block to have a new or hard-to-find Beanie, and you will be well rewarded for having patience. Even if a Beanie retires quickly, you're better off spending your money knowing the Beanie is retired rather than trying to buy it for a premium price. Otherwise, you're taking a chance that Beanie may be out for years, becoming as common as any other.

The estimated values listed in this guide are based on the *latest available version* of the Beanie Baby. Earlier versions are almost always worth more money.

All markets, be they stocks or Beanies, have price corrections and points of resistance. The trick is in finding a pattern to the corrections and using them to your advantage. The hard part of that is that Beanies haven't been around long enough to determine a sure pattern. This uncertainty is actually helping to feed the Beanie market right now. As for collecting, always follow the primary rule: Don't collect anything you don't like. That way, whatever happens to the market, you will always have something you can enjoy.

1998 Spring Arrivals

Ants
(the anteater)

Most anteaters love to eat bugs
But this little fellow gives big hugs
He'd rather dine on apple pie
Than eat an ant or harm a fly!

BIRTHDAY: NOVEMBER 7, 1997
DATE RELEASED: MAY 30, 1998
DATE RETIRED: (CURRENT)
STYLE # 4195
HANG TAG GENERATION: 5

Fetch
(the Golden Retriever)

Fetch is alert at the crack of dawn
Walking through dewdrops on the lawn
Always golden, loyal and true
This little puppy is the one for you!

BIRTHDAY: FEBRUARY 4, 1997
DATE RELEASED: MAY 30, 1998
DATE RETIRED: (CURRENT)
STYLE # 4189
HANG TAG GENERATION: 5

Early
(the robin)

Early is a red breasted robin
For worms he'll soon be bobbin'
Known as a sign of spring
This happy robin loves to sing!

BIRTHDAY: FEBRUARY 20, 1997
DATE RELEASED: MAY 30, 1998
DATE RETIRED: (CURRENT)
STYLE # 4190
HANG TAG GENERATION: 5

Fortune
(the panda)

Nibbling on a bamboo tree
This little panda is hard to see
You're so lucky with this one you found
Only a few are still around!

BIRTHDAY: DECEMBER 6, 1997
DATE RELEASED: MAY 30, 1998
DATE RETIRED: (CURRENT)
STYLE # 4196
HANG TAG GENERATION: 5

Gigi
(the Poodle)

Prancing and dancing all down
the street
Thinking her hairdo is oh, so neat
Always so careful in the wind
and rain
She's a dog that's anything but
plain

BIRTHDAY: MARCH 7, 1997
DATE RELEASED: MAY 30, 1998
DATE RETIRED: (CURRENT)
STYLE # 4191
HANG TAG GENERATION: 5

Jabber
(the parrot)

Teaching Jabber to move his
beak
A large vocabulary he now can
speak
Jabber will repeat what you say
Teach him a new word every
day!

BIRTHDAY: OCTOBER 10, 1997
DATE RELEASED: MAY 30, 1998
DATE RETIRED: (CURRENT)
STYLE # 4197
HANG TAG GENERATION: 5

Glory
(the bear)

Oh say can you see
Glory's proud of her country
Born on Independence Day
This bear lives in the USA!

BIRTHDAY: JULY 4, 1997
DATE RELEASED: MAY 30, 1998
DATE RETIRED: (CURRENT)
STYLE # 4188
HANG TAG GENERATION: 5

Jake
(the mallard duck)

Jake the drake likes to splash
in a puddle
Take him home and give him a
cuddle
Quack, Quack, Quack, he will say
He's so glad you're here to play!

BIRTHDAY: APRIL 16, 1997
DATE RELEASED: MAY 30, 1998
DATE RETIRED: (CURRENT)
STYLE # 4199
HANG TAG GENERATION: 5

Rocket
(the blue jay)

Rocket is the fastest blue jay
ever
He flies in all sorts of weather
Aerial tricks are his specialty
He's so entertaining for you
and me!

BIRTHDAY: MARCH 12,
1997
DATE RELEASED: MAY
30, 1998
DATE RETIRED:
(CURRENT)
STYLE # 4202
HANG TAG GENERATION: 5

Kuku
(the cockatoo)

This fancy bird loves to
converse
He talks in poems, rhythms and
verse
So take him home and give him
some time
You'll be suprised how he can
rhyme

BIRTHDAY: JANUARY 5, 1997
DATE RELEASED: MAY 30,
1998
DATE RETIRED: (CURRENT)
STYLE # 4192
HANG TAG GENERATION: 5

Stinger
(the scorpion)

Stinger the scorpion will run
and dart
But this little fellow is
really all heart
so if you see him
don't run away
Say hello and
ask him to play!

BIRTHDAY: SEPTEMBER
29, 1997
DATE RELEASED: MAY 30, 1998
DATE RETIRED: (CURRENT)
STYLE # 4193
HANG TAG GENERATION: 5

Tracker
(the Basset Hound)

Sniffing and tracking and
following trails
Tracker the bassett always wags
his tail
It doesn't matter what you do
He's always happy he's with you

Birthday: June 5, 1997
Date Released: May 30, 1998
Date Retired: (current)
Style # 4198
Hang Tag Generation: 5

Wise
(the owl)

With A's and B's he'll always
pass
Wise is the head of the class
He's got his diploma and feels
really great
Meet the newest graduate:
Class of '98!

Birthday: May 31, 1997
Date Released: May 30, 1998
Date Retired: (current)
Style # 4194
Hang Tag Generation: 5

Whisper
(the deer)

She's very shy as you can see
When she hides behind a tree
With big brown eyes and soft to touch
This little fawn will love you so
much!

Birthday: April 5, 1997
Date Released: May 30, 1998
Date Retired: (current)
Style # 4187
Hang Tag Generation: 5

Beanie Babies Checklist

- [ ] 1997 Holiday Teddy
- [ ] Ally the alligator
- [x] Ants the anteater
- [x] Baldy the eagle
- [x] Batty the bat
- [x] Bernie the St. Bernard
- [x] Bessie the cow
- [x] Blackie the bear
- [x] Blizzard the tiger
- [x] Bones the dog
- [x] Bongo the monkey
- [ ] Britannia the bear
- [ ] Bronty the brontosaurus
- [ ] Brownie the bear
- [x] Bruno the terrier
- [ ] Bubbles the fish
- [x] Bucky the beaver
- [ ] Bumble the bee
- [ ] Caw the crow
- [ ] Chilly the polar bear
- [x] Chip the calico cat
- [x] Chocolate the moose
- [ ] Chops the lamb
- [x] Claude the crab
- [x] Congo the gorilla
- [ ] Coral the fish
- [x] Crunch the shark
- [x] Cubbie the bear
- [x] Curly the bear
- [x] Daisy the cow
- [x] Derby the horse
  - [ ] (coarse mane)
  - [ ] (fine mane)
  - [ ] (white star)
- Digger the crab
  - [ ] (orange)
  - [ ] (red)
- [x] Doby the Doberman
- [ ] Doodle the rooster
- [x] Dotty the Dalmatian
- [x] Early the robin
- [x] Ears the brown rabbit
- [x] Echo the dolphin
- [x] Erin the bear
- [x] Fetch the Golden Retriever
- [x] Flash the dolphin
- [x] Fleece the lamb
- [x] Flip the white cat
- [x] Floppity the lilac bunny
- [ ] Flutter the butterfly
- [x] Fortune the panda
- [x] Freckles the leopard

24

- [ ] Garcia the bear
- [x] Gigi the Poodle
- [x] Glory the bear
- [x] Gobbles the turkey
- [x] Goldie the goldfish
- [x] Gracie the swan
- [ ] Grunt the razorback

Happy the hippo
- [ ] (gray)
- [x] (lavender)

- [x] Hippity the mint bunny
- [x] Hissy the snake
- [x] Hoot the owl
- [x] Hoppity the rose bunny
- [ ] Humphrey the camel
- [x] Iggy the iguana

Inch the inchworm
- [ ] (felt antennae)
- [ ] (yarn antennae)

Inky the octopus
- [ ] (pink)
- [ ] (tan, no mouth)
- [ ] (tan, with mouth)

- [x] Jabber the parrot
- [x] Jake the mallard duck

- [x] Jolly the walrus
- [x] Kiwi the toucan
- [x] Kuku the cockatoo
- [ ] Lefty the donkey
- [x] Legs the frog
- [ ] Libearty the bear

Lizzy the lizard
- [ ] (blue)
- [ ] (tie-dyed)

Lucky the ladybug
- [ ] (7 spots)
- [ ] (11 spots)
- [ ] (21 spots)

- [x] Magic the dragon
- [x] Manny the manatee
- [ ] Maple the bear
- [x] Mel the koala

Mystic the unicorn
- [ ] (coarse mane)
- [ ] (fine mane)
- [ ] (iridescent horn)

- [ ] Nana the monkey
- [x] Nanook the Husky

Nip the gold cat
- [ ] (all gold)
- [ ] (white face and belly)

25

- [ ] (white paws)
- [x] Nuts the squirrel
- Patti the platypus ✗
  - [ ] (deep fuschia)
  - [ ] (fuschia)
  - [ ] (magenta)
  - [ ] (raspberry)
- [x] Peace the bear
- Peanut the elephant
  - [x] (light blue)
  - [ ] (royal blue)
- [ ] Peking the panda
- [x] Pinchers the lobster
- [x] Pinky the flamingo
- [x] Pouch the kangaroo
- [x] Pounce the cat
- [ ] Prance the cat
- [ ] Princess the bear
- [x] Puffer the puffin
- [x] Pugsly the Pug
- [x] Punchers the lobster ˢᵐ
- Quackers the duck
  - [x] (with wings)
  - [ ] (without wings)
- [ ] Radar the bat
- [x] Rainbow the chameleon

- [ ] Rex the tyrannosaurus
- [ ] Righty the elephant
- [x] Ringo the raccoon
- [x] Roary the lion
- [x] Rocket the blue jay
- [x] Rover the dog
- [x] Scoop the pelican ˢᵐ
- [x] Scottie the Scottish Terrier
- [ ] Seamore the seal
- [x] Seaweed the otter
- [ ] Slither the snake
- Sly the fox ✗
  - [ ] (brown belly)
  - [ ] (white belly)
- [x] Smoochy the frog
- [x] Snip the Siamese cat
- [x] Snort the bull
- [ ] Snowball the snowman
- [x] Sparky the Dalmatian
- [x] Speedy the turtle
- [x] Spike the rhinoceros
- [ ] Spinner the spider
- [x] Splash the whale
- [x] Spooky the ghost
- Spot the dog
  - [x] (with spot)

☐ (no spot)
☒ Spunky the Cocker Spaniel
☒ Squealer the pig
☐ Steg the stegosaurus
☐ Sting the stingray
☒ Stinger the scorpion
☒ Stinky the skunk
☒ Stretch the ostrich
✗ Stripes the tiger
  ☐ (dark)
  ☐ (light)
☒ Strut the rooster
☐ Tabasco the bull
Tank the armadillo
  ☐ (nine lines)
  ☐ (nine lines, no shell)
  ☐ (seven lines, no shell)
Teddy the new-faced bear
  ☐ (brown)
  ☐ (cranberry)
  ☐ (jade)
  ☐ (magenta)
  ☐ (teal)
  ☐ (violet)

Teddy the old-faced bear
  ☐ (brown)
  ☐ (cranberry)
  ☐ (jade)
  ☐ (magenta)
  ☐ (teal)
  ☐ (violet)
☒ Tracker the Basset Hound
☐ Trap the mouse
☒ Tuffy the terrier
☒ Tusk the walrus
☒ Twigs the giraffe
☒ Valentino the bear
☒ Velvet the panther
☒ Waddle the penguin
☒ Waves the whale
☐ Web the spider
☒ Weenie the Dachshund
☐ Wise the owl
☒ Wrinkles the Bulldog
☒ Ziggy the zebra
✗ Zip the black cat
  ☐ (all black)
  ☐ (white face and belly)
  ☐ (white paws)

27

1997
Holiday Teddy

Beanie Babies are
special no doubt
All filled with love -
inside and out
Wishes for fun times
filled with joy
Ty's holiday teddy is a
magical toy!

BIRTHDAY: DECEMBER 25, 1996
DATE RELEASED: OCTOBER 1, 1997
DATE RETIRED: DECEMBER 31, 1997
STYLE # 4200
HANG TAG GENERATION: 4
ESTIMATED VALUE: $35–$45

The 1997 Holiday Teddy resembles the new-faced brown Teddy,
but his fur is more caramel-colored than brown. When a picture of
this little bear first appeared on the Ty website, he had green and
red bows on his neck, but collectors will usually find him wearing a
red scarf with white fringe. The 1997 Teddy was retired on December 31, 1997, after only three months in Beaniedom. Given the short
amount of time he remained on the market and the fact he was
retired before many collectors were able to find him, his value
should increase tremendously. It seems that he may be the first in
an annual series of Beanies, which will also help his value.

Ally
(the alligator)

When Ally gets out of
classes
He wears a hat and dark
glasses
He plays bass in a street
band
He's the coolest gator in
the land!

BIRTHDAY: MARCH 14, 1994
DATE RELEASED: JUNE 25, 1994
DATE RETIRED: OCTOBER 1, 1997
STYLE # 4032
HANG TAG GENERATION: 1–4
ESTIMATED VALUE: $35–$45

Avocado Ally appeared with the second release of Beanies and was never redesigned during his time as a current. It's extremely difficult to find intact first- and second-generation hang tags on Ally, probably because children loved to play with him from the get-go. Devoted Beanie collectors covet him all the same—mint tags, beat-up tags, or no tags! Due to his long reign as a current, Ally can be found fairly easily on the secondary market, so now is a good time to pick him up at a reasonable price.

Baldy
(the eagle)

Hair on his head is quite scant
We suggest Baldy get a transplant
Watching over the land of the free
Hair in his eyes would make it hard to see!

BIRTHDAY: FEBRUARY 17, 1996
DATE RELEASED: MAY 11, 1997
DATE RETIRED: MAY 1, 1998
STYLE # 4074
HANG TAG GENERATION: 4–5
ESTIMATED VALUE: $12–$15

On Baldy's original release on May 11, 1996, his name was printed in all capital letters on the inside of his fourth-generation hang tag. (This error was also found on Tuffy the terrier and Claude the crab in the May 11, 1997, release.) Baldy, the first of the professional-basketball Beanies, was used in a special promotion in conjunction with the Philadelphia 76ers of the NBA in January 1998. Being our national symbol, Baldy fit in perfectly in the City of Brotherly Love. Retired after less than a year, Baldy may become one of the more valuable May 1998 retirees.

Batty
(the bat)

Bats may make some
people jitter
Please don't be scared
of this critter
If you're lonely or have
nothing to do
This Beanie Baby would
love to hug you!

BIRTHDAY: OCTOBER 29, 1996
DATE RELEASED: OCTOBER 1, 1997
DATE RETIRED: (CURRENT)
STYLE # 4035
HANG TAG GENERATION: 4–5
ESTIMATED VALUE: $5–$7

The second bat in the Beanie Babies line, Batty was a fitting replacement for the retired Radar. With his wings wrapped around him, Batty becomes one of the smallest Beanies around. Batty's plush is a pinkish-brown color, but this Beanie's most interesting feature is the Velcro hook-and-loop fasteners on the tips of his wings. The Velcro allows Batty to be wrapped around another Beanie or strapped on a child's wrist like a bracelet. Despite many people's feelings of distaste toward bats, Batty has proved extremely popular—probably due to his unusual wings.

Bernie
(the St. Bernard)

This little dog can't wait to grow
To rescue people lost in the snow
Don't let him out - keep him on your shelf
He doesn't know how to rescue himself!

BIRTHDAY: OCTOBER 3, 1996
DATE RELEASED: JANUARY 1, 1997
DATE RETIRED: (CURRENT)
STYLE # 4109
HANG TAG GENERATION: 4–5
ESTIMATED VALUE: $5–$7

Bernie is a member of the Beanie dogs—one of the most popular Beanie "groups." Bernie (along with Doby the Doberman) was among the second release of purebreds—dogs who carry their breed as part of their name. Many of the previous releases, such as Spot and Rover, didn't belong to any specific breed. Bernie's sad eyes and upturned face appeal to collectors of all ages and really seem to fit his slightly sad poem. Collectors who are fans of the movie *Beethoven* and its sequel will want a whole litter of Bernies.

Bessie
(the cow)

Bessie the cow likes to
dance and sing
Because music is her
favorite thing
Every night when you
are counting sheep
She'll sing you a song to
help you sleep!

BIRTHDAY: JUNE 27, 1995
DATE RELEASED: JUNE 3, 1995
DATE RETIRED: OCTOBER 1, 1997
STYLE # 4009
HANG TAG GENERATION: 2–4
ESTIMATED VALUE: $50–$60

Bessie has had two different colors of horns: The horns on the earlier Bessies were a little darker than the horns on the more recent Bessies. Even though Bessie had been around since June 1995, her retirement in October 1997 caught many collectors by surprise. Daisy, the black cow, had been out a year longer, so most expected Daisy to be sent out to pasture first. As a result, many collectors still need Bessie to complete their collections, and her value has increased more than that of the average Beanie. Notice anything odd about Bessie's birthday? It's after her release date!

Blackie
(the bear)

Living in a national park
He only played after dark
Then he met his friend Cubbie
Now they play when it's sunny!

BIRTHDAY: JULY 15, 1994
DATE RELEASED: JUNE 25, 1994
DATE RETIRED: (CURRENT)
STYLE # 4011
HANG TAG GENERATION: 1–5
ESTIMATED VALUE: $5–$7

With Blackie's friend Cubbie already retired, will Blackie be far behind? Only Ty can answer that question for sure, but Blackie is now the only remaining lay down–style bear. Blackie was one of the group of Beanies shipped in January 1998 whose fifth-generation hang tags had the word "original" spelled "origiinal" on the front and had the "r" left out of "surface" on the back. Look for these errors on the bunny trio of Floppity, Hippity, and Hoppity, as well as on Curly, Peace, and Valentino the bears.

Blizzard

(the tiger)

In the mountains, where
it's snowy and cold
Lives a beautiful tiger,
I've been told
Black and white, she's
hard to compare
Of all the tigers, she is
most rare!

BIRTHDAY: DECEMBER 12, 1996
DATE RELEASED: MAY 11, 1997
DATE RETIRED: MAY 1, 1998
STYLE # 4163
HANG TAG GENERATION: 4–5
ESTIMATED VALUE: $12–$15

So many rumors! Ever since Ty had to change Doodle's name to Strut because of a potential trademark infringement, collectors were convinced that Blizzard would be retired in October 1997. Therefore, she became very hard to find. At one point, there were even pictures distributed of Blizzard with a "Snowball" hang tag, but those turned out to be forgeries. Finally, the premonitions came true on May 1, 1998, when Blizzard was retired, but it's hard to say whether her retirement was caused by trademark problems, or if it was simply Ty's decision.

Bones
(the dog)

**Bones is a dog that
loves to chew
Chairs and tables and a
smelly old shoe
"You're so destructive"
all would shout
But that all stopped,
when his teeth fell out!**

BIRTHDAY: JANUARY 18, 1994
DATE RELEASED: JUNE 25, 1994
DATE RETIRED: MAY 1, 1998
STYLE # 4001
HANG TAG GENERATION: 1–5
ESTIMATED VALUE: $12–$15

Bones was the second Beanie Babies dog to be released. (Spot, one of the original nine Beanies, was the first.) Most people think Bones is just a mutt, but it's likely he's modeled after a Bloodhound. Bones is the Beanie everyone thinks of as being a "Pound Puppy," from the popular children's toy series that appeared several years before Beanies were introduced to the world. Look for Teenie Bones in the second McDonald's collection. Bones's retirement, combined with his Teenie namesake, will help his value over time.
Teenie Beanie (second set)

Bongo
(the monkey)

Bongo the monkey lives
in a tree
The happiest monkey
you'll ever see
In his spare time he
plays the guitar
One of these days he
will be a big star!

(tan-tailed Nana)
BIRTHDAY: (NONE)
DATE RELEASED: JUNE 3, 1995
DATE RETIRED: (UNKNOWN)
STYLE # 4067
HANG TAG GENERATION: 3
ESTIMATED VALUE: $3,500–$4,000

(brown tail)
BIRTHDAY: AUGUST 17, 1995
DATE RELEASED: FEBRUARY 6, 1996
DATE RETIRED: JUNE 29, 1996
STYLE # 4067
HANG TAG GENERATION: 3–4
ESTIMATED VALUE: $50–$60

(tan-tailed Bongo)
BIRTHDAY: AUGUST 17, 1995
DATE RELEASED: JUNE 3, 1995
DATE RETIRED: (CURRENT)
STYLE # 4067
HANG TAG GENERATION: 3–5
ESTIMATED VALUE: $5–$7

Bongo was originally released with the name Nana. Nana is one of the rarest Beanies around. Interestingly, some Bongos were Nanas once upon a time: The name Bongo was taped over the name Nana on the tag! Bongo has been released with a tan tail as well as a brown tail that matches his body. The tag generation, combined with the tail color, is what affects his value.
Teenie Beanie (second set)

Britannia
(the bear)

Britannia the bear will
sail the sea
So she can be with you
and me
She's always sure to
catch the tide
And wear the Union Flag
with pride

BIRTHDAY: DECEMBER 15, 1997
DATE RELEASED: DECEMBER 31, 1997
DATE RETIRED: (CURRENT)
STYLE # 4601
HANG TAG GENERATION: 5
ESTIMATED VALUE: $10–$20

Britannia (along with Righty, Lefty, Libearty, Maple, and Glory) is one of the growing number of "patriotic" Beanies. With a Union Jack embroidered on her chest, she is available in shops only in the United Kingdom, making her all the more desirable to collectors in the United States. If her flag is missing (as has been the case on other Beanies with embroidery or flags), it's hard to tell at a glance whether it's Teddy the new-faced brown bear or Britannia.

Bronty
(the brontosaurus)

(No poem)

BIRTHDAY: (NONE)
DATE RELEASED: JUNE 3, 1995
DATE RETIRED: JUNE 15, 1996
STYLE # 4085
HANG TAG GENERATION: 3
ESTIMATED VALUE: $850–$1,000

Poor Bronty! Released too early and retired too soon to even have a birthday or a poem, his beautiful blue tie-dyed plush (the same as Sting the stingray's) makes up for this slight. Every Bronty is just a little different from the next one, and collectors are always on the lookout for a tie-dye pattern that appeals to them. A mint-condition Bronty is very hard to find and commands a premium price. This extinct Beanie is a great addition to any collection. An interesting fact: Bronty shares a style number with Righty the elephant.

Bruno
(the terrier)

Bruno the dog thinks
he's a brute
But all the other Beanies
think he's cute
He growls at his tail and
runs in a ring
And everyone says, "Oh,
how darling!"

BIRTHDAY: SEPTEMBER 9, 1997
DATE RELEASED: DECEMBER 31, 1997
DATE RETIRED: (CURRENT)
STYLE # 4183
HANG TAG GENERATION: 5
ESTIMATED VALUE: $5–$7

When brutish Bruno was first released, his picture didn't do him justice. A lot of people didn't think much of him until he started appearing in stores, at which point people changed their tune and clamored to take the cute pup home. Bruno has a long, rounded, brown-and-white nose and solid, muscular-looking body, just like the dog after which he's modeled—a Bull Terrier! As part of the Beanie Babies dog group, Bruno has been a popular buy.

Bubbles
(the fish)

All day long Bubbles
likes to swim
She never gets tired of
flapping her fins
Bubbles lived in a sea
of blue
Now she is ready to
come home with you!

BIRTHDAY: JULY 2, 1995
DATE RELEASED: JUNE 3, 1995
DATE RETIRED: MAY 11, 1997
STYLE # 4078
HANG TAG GENERATION: 3–4
ESTIMATED VALUE: $120–$150

With her black-and-yellow stripes, it's no wonder Bubbles's name is similar to Bumble the bee's. Bubbles was the second of the fish trio (Coral and Goldie are the other fish) to be retired. She swam into the Beanie pond at the same time as Coral but, unlike Coral, was around after the Teenie Beanies reeled in countless new Beanie collectors. Many of them were lucky enough to be able to add Bubbles to their collections before she retired a few weeks later. Beware of Bubbles bearing a Grunt tush tag! Chances are it's a counterfeit.

Bucky
(the beaver)

Bucky's teeth are shiny
as can be
Often used for cutting
trees
He hides in his dam
night and day
Maybe for you he will
come out and play!

BIRTHDAY: JUNE 8, 1995
DATE RELEASED: JANUARY 7, 1996
DATE RETIRED: DECEMBER 31, 1997
STYLE # 4016
HANG TAG GENERATION: 3–4
ESTIMATED VALUE: $30–$40

Nobody knows exactly what prompted the retirement of this toothy Beanie. Bucky shares the same basic body shape with Ringo the racoon, Sly the fox, and Stinky the skunk, and some collectors figured Ty thought that was too many Beanies with the same shape. Others thought it was because Bucky was one of the less-popular Beanies. If that's really true, Bucky may turn out to be a great investment for those just starting to collect retireds because of his still-inexpensive price. Now may be a good time to pick him up!

Bumble
(the bee)

Bumble the bee will not
sting you
It is only love that this
bee will bring you
So don't be afraid to
give this bee a hug
Because Bumble the bee
is a love-bug.

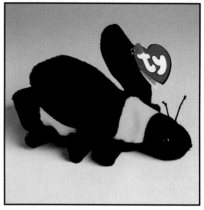

BIRTHDAY: OCTOBER 16,1995
DATE RELEASED: JUNE 3, 1995
DATE RETIRED: JUNE 15, 1996
STYLE # 4045
HANG TAG GENERATION: 3–4
ESTIMATED VALUE: $550–$650

Bumble, one of the smallest Beanies, can fit easily into the palm of
your hand. Bumble is an exception to the Beanie Babies "rule" of
older tags being more valuable than newer tags. He is the only
Beanie from the June 15, 1996, retirement that was shipped with
fourth-generation hang tags and a poem. Don't be fooled if someone
tells you the older tag is worth more money on this little bee: This is
the only Beanie on which a fourth-generation tag is actually more
valuable than a third-generation tag.

Caw
(the crow)

(No poem)

BIRTHDAY: (NONE)
DATE RELEASED: JUNE 3, 1995
DATE RETIRED: JUNE 15, 1996
STYLE # 4071
HANG TAG GENERATION: 3
ESTIMATED VALUE: $600–$700

Because of Caw's bright orange beak and webbed feet, he is often referred to as a "black duck." This crow isn't very well known outside of Beanie collecting circles. Lucky collectors may be able to find him at a flea market or a garage sale, even without a hang tag, for much less than his going value. The Korean-made Caws are often much plumper than Caws made in China, which is where most Beanies are made. Caw doesn't carry quite as high a price tag as some of the other, older retireds.

Chilly
(the polar bear)

(No poem)

BIRTHDAY: (NONE)
DATE RELEASED: JUNE 25, 1994
DATE RETIRED: JANUARY 7, 1996
STYLE # 4012
HANG TAG GENERATION: 1–3
ESTIMATED VALUE: $1,750–$2,000

Chilly was one of the first Beanies to increase substantially in value. As an early Beanie, he was a favorite toy for many children before Beanies became collectible. He's very difficult to find in anything close to mint condition because, like all the white plush Beanies, he gets dirty very easily. Along with Blackie, Peking, and Cubbie, he is one of the four lay down–style bears. Chilly's style number was reused on the also-all-white Flip the cat.

Chip
(the calico cat)

Black and gold, brown
and white
The shades of her coat
are quite a sight
At mixing her colors she
was a master
On anyone else it would
be a disaster!

BIRTHDAY: JANUARY 26, 1996
DATE RELEASED: MAY 1, 1997
DATE RETIRED: (CURRENT)
STYLE # 4121
HANG TAG GENERATION: 4–5
ESTIMATED VALUE: $5–$7

Calico cats, like Chip, are almost always female. The genes that make cats calico are part of the same genes that make cats female. The Beanie Babies cat group is generally second in popularity to the Beanie dogs, but since Ty has released fewer cats than dogs in the Beanie family, any new cat is automatically considered a "must-have." Chip was very hard to find when she was first released; she was the only cat in a release that included four dogs: Dotty, Nanook, Pugsly, and Tuffy.

Chocolate
(the moose)

Licorice, gum and
peppermint candy
This moose always has
these handy
But there is one more
thing he likes to eat
Can you guess his
favorite sweet?

BIRTHDAY: APRIL 27, 1993
DATE RELEASED: JANUARY 8, 1994
DATE RETIRED: (CURRENT)
STYLE # 4015
HANG TAG GENERATION: 1–5
ESTIMATED VALUE: $5–$7

Chocolate was one of the original nine Beanies introduced in
January 1994, and is "mom" to one of the original McDonald's
Teenie Beanies. He is the only remaining current of the original
nine. Chocolate's clever name has made him extremely popular
among older collectors. Young collectors just love his floppy orange
antlers and "bemoosed" expression. On Chocolates with a fourth-
generation hang tag, check to see if the word "moose" appears as
the typo "rnoose." Older tags are very hard to find, and when
Chocolate retires, they'll become valuable quickly!
Teenie Beanie (first set)

47

Chops
(the lamb)

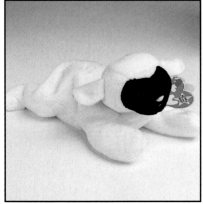

Chops is a little lamb
This lamb you'll surely
know
Because every path that
you may take
This lamb is sure to go!

BIRTHDAY: MAY 3, 1996
DATE RELEASED: JANUARY 7, 1996
DATE RETIRED: JANUARY 1, 1997
STYLE # 4019
HANG TAG GENERATION: 3–4
ESTIMATED VALUE: $140–$180

Sweet little Chops was only out a year before her retirement in January 1997. She may have been retired because her name too closely matched that of Sherry Lewis's puppet, Lamb Chop. It's almost certain that Chops's retirement was unplanned, because she was the only McDonald's Teenie Beanie "mom" already retired when the Teenies first came out in April 1997. The combination of her moderately early retirement and her status as a "mom" makes it quite likely that her value will increase significantly. Note the misspelling of the word "surely" in some of Chops's tags!
Teenie Beanie (first set)

Claude
(the crab)

Claude the crab paints
by the sea
A famous artist he hopes
to be
But the tide came in and
his paints fell
Now his art is on his
shell!

BIRTHDAY: SEPTEMBER 3, 1996
DATE RELEASED: MAY 11, 1997
DATE RETIRED: (CURRENT)
STYLE # 4083
HANG TAG GENERATION: 4–5
ESTIMATED VALUE: $5–$7

Claude was presented to the world at the same time the previous crab, Digger, was retired. Claude, a tie-dyed Beanie, became popular immediately, though his tie-dyed colors are far more muted than those of tie-dyes like Coral the fish, Garcia the bear, Flutter the butterfly, and Peace the bear. Collectors lucky enough to own an early Claude should check his hang tag to see if his name is spelled in all capital letters. This error appeared on only a few Beanies and makes them even more valuable.

Congo
(the gorilla)

Black as the night and
fierce is he
On the ground or in a
tree
Strong and mighty as the
Congo
He's related to our
Bongo!

BIRTHDAY: NOVEMBER 9, 1996
DATE RELEASED: JUNE 15, 1996
DATE RETIRED: (CURRENT)
STYLE # 4160
HANG TAG GENERATION: 4–5
ESTIMATED VALUE: $5–$7

Like Bessie the cow, Congo's birthday is actually after his release
date! But, unlike Bessie, Congo comes with a fourth-generation (or
later) hang tag that originally had a birthday and a poem. Congo is
a great addition to any Beanie collection, and the nice thing about
him is that collectors don't have to go bananas when looking for
him: He's still readily available. Congo was used as a promotion at
the 1998 Toy Fair in New York City, where showgoers and Beanie
collectors alike went ape over him.

Coral
(the fish)

Coral is beautiful, as you
know
Made of colors in the
rainbow
Whether it's pink, yellow
or blue
These colors were
chosen just for you!

BIRTHDAY: MARCH 2, 1995
DATE RELEASED: JUNE 3, 1995
DATE RETIRED: JANUARY 1, 1997
STYLE # 4079
HANG TAG GENERATION: 3–4
ESTIMATED VALUE: $150–$180

The neat thing about Coral and the rest of the tie-dye Beanies is
that each one is unique. Because each one has a different color and
different pattern, in an entire school of Corals, no two would look
the same. The tie-dye Beanies—whether current or retired—are
very popular, but since Coral retired before the Teenie Beanies
brought in a whole new school of collectors, she's in demand for
that reason, too.

Crunch
(the shark)

What's for breakfast?
What's for lunch?
Yum! Delicious! Munch,
munch, munch!
He's eating everything
by the bunch
That's the reason we
named him Crunch!

BIRTHDAY: JANUARY 13, 1996
DATE RELEASED: JANUARY 1, 1997
DATE RETIRED: (CURRENT)
STYLE # 4130
HANG TAG GENERATION: 4–5
ESTIMATED VALUE: $5–$7

Because of potential conflicts with both a cereal name and the name of a chocolate bar, Crunch is another Beanie about whom rumors run wild. Crunch has appeared on "Top 10" retirement lists almost since his introduction in January 1997. Definitely more popular with boys than he is with girls, this shark looks surprisingly realistic. Just when you thought it was safe to go back into the water...!

Cubbie
(the bear)

Cubbie used to eat
crackers and honey
And what happened to
him was funny
He was stung by
fourteen bees
Now Cubbie eats broccoli
and cheese!

(Brownie)	*(Cubbie)*
BIRTHDAY: (NONE)	BIRTHDAY: NOVEMBER 14, 1993
DATE RELEASED: 1993	DATE RELEASED: JANUARY 8, 1994
DATE RETIRED: PRIOR TO JAN. 8, 1994	DATE RETIRED: DECEMBER 31, 1997
STYLE # 4010	STYLE # 4010
HANG TAG GENERATION: 1	HANG TAG GENERATION: 1–4
ESTIMATED VALUE: $3,750–$4,000	ESTIMATED VALUE: $22–$30

One of the original nine Beanies, Cubbie was first released with the
name Brownie. The only difference between Brownie and Cubbie is
the name tag, so don't let someone convince you their Brownie is
missing his hang tag: If there's not a first-generation hang tag that
says Brownie, you're looking at Cubbie. A few Cubbies with fifth-
generation hang tags snuck out of hibernation before Cubbie was
retired; this fifth-generation Cubbie will be worth a little more on
the secondary market than other generations. Cubbie became the
first sports-promotion Beanie on May 18, 1997, for the Chicago
Cubs.

Curly
(the bear)

A bear so cute with hair
that's Curly
You will love and want
him surely
To this bear always be
true
He will be a friend to
you!

BIRTHDAY: APRIL 12, 1996
DATE RELEASED: JUNE 15, 1996
DATE RETIRED: (CURRENT)
STYLE # 4052
HANG TAG GENERATION: 4–5
ESTIMATED VALUE: $5–$7

Curly was one of the first two Beanies with "napped" fur rather than the plush fur found on the others. Scottie the Scottish Terrier, also with napped fur, was released at the same time — June 1996. Watch for an error on Curly's tag in which "surely" is spelled "surly" in the poem. Like some of the other Beanies with fifth-generation tags, the word "original" was spelled "origiinal" on his tag. Curly, who is always a favorite in the retirement rumor mill, shares a style number with the cranberry old- and new-faced Teddies.

Daisy
(the cow)

Daisy drinks milk each
night
So her coat is shiny and
bright
Milk is good for your hair
and skin
What a way for your day
to begin!

BIRTHDAY: MAY 10, 1994
DATE RELEASED: JUNE 25, 1994
DATE RETIRED: (CURRENT)
STYLE # 4006
HANG TAG GENERATION: 1–5
ESTIMATED VALUE: $5–$7

One of the few Beanies who have survived all five generations of
hang tags, Daisy was designed as a lay down–style cow, while her
cow-nterpart, Bessie, was designed as a "sit-up" cow. The white
spot on Daisy's back is a mirror image of Spot the dog's black spot.
On very rare occasions, a spotless Daisy can be found as well.
Daisy is only the second "special edition" Beanie with a specially
printed second hang tag. The special tag honors the late Chicago
Cubs announcer Harry Caray with a special poem and a caricature
of Harry.

Derby
(the horse)

All the other horses
used to tattle
Because Derby never
wore his saddle
He left the stables,
and the horses too
Just so Derby can be
with you!

(fine mane)
BIRTHDAY: SEPTEMBER 16, 1995
DATE RELEASED: JUNE 3, 1995
DATE RETIRED: (UNKNOWN)
STYLE # 4008
HANG TAG GENERATION: 3
ESTIMATED VALUE: $2,750–$3,250

(coarse mane)
BIRTHDAY: SEPTEMBER 16, 1995
DATE RELEASED: (UNKNOWN)
DATE RETIRED: DECEMBER 15, 1997
STYLE # 4008
HANG TAG GENERATION: 4–5
ESTIMATED VALUE: $20–$25

(with star)
BIRTHDAY: SEPTEMBER 16, 1995
DATE RELEASED: DECEMBER 15, 1997
DATE RETIRED: (CURRENT)
STYLE # 4008
HANG TAG GENERATION: 5
ESTIMATED VALUE: $5–$7

Derby has been redesigned into three distinct Beanies. In the first
version, the mane and tail were made out of thinner yarn. This
limited-production Derby was only available with the third-generation hang tag. The second version features thicker yarn on the mane
and tail. Still another Derby appeared in 1998; this one has a white
star on his forehead and has fifth-generation tags only.

56

Digger

(the crab)

Digging in the sand and
walking sideways
That's how Digger
spends her days
Hard on the outside but
sweet deep inside
Basking in the sun and
riding the tide!

(orange)	**(red)**
BIRTHDAY: AUGUST 23, 1995	BIRTHDAY: AUGUST 23, 1995
DATE RELEASED: JUNE 25, 1994	DATE RELEASED: JUNE 3, 1995
DATE RETIRED: JUNE 3, 1995	DATE RETIRED: MAY 11, 1997
STYLE # 4027	STYLE # 4027
HANG TAG GENERATION: 1–3	HANG TAG GENERATION: 3–4
ESTIMATED VALUE: $750–$850	ESTIMATED VALUE: $100–$125

Released with the second group of Beanies in mid-1994, the original
Digger was bright orange, just like Chocolate the moose's antlers.
This orange Digger can be seen wearing the first three generations
of hang tags. He was on the market about a year before he was
redesigned into the better-known red Digger (third- and fourth-
generation tags). As retired Beanies go, red Digger is still a pretty
good bargain. Now would be a good time to find one. Orange
Digger is really quite stunning, but as an older retired, sadly, he's
not as affordable.

Doby
(the Doberman)

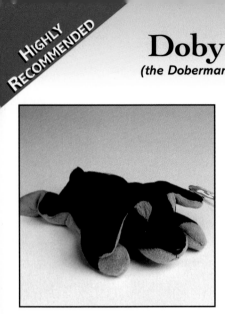

This dog is little but he has might
Keep him close when you sleep at night
He lays around with nothing to do
Until he sees its time to protect you!

BIRTHDAY: OCTOBER 9, 1996
DATE RELEASED: JANUARY 1, 1997
DATE RETIRED: (CURRENT)
STYLE # 4110
HANG TAG GENERATION: 4–5
ESTIMATED VALUE: $5–$7

Oh, what excitement one little dog can bring! When McDonald's announced a second set of Teenie Beanies to be released in May 1998, trying to guess which Beanies would become Teenie Beanies became a top priority among collectors. And then Teenie Doby appeared at a swap meet in his teenie bag with a large "No. 1" on it! The question of which Teenie would be first was answered, and the rush was on to pick up Doby in order to have matching "moms" and Teenie Babies. The grammatical error (*its* instead of *it's*) in Doby's poem has not affected his worth.
Teenie Beanie (second set)

Doodle
(the rooster)

Listen closely to "cock-a-doodle-doo"
What's the rooster saying to you?
Hurry, wake up sleepy head
We have lots to do, get out of bed!

BIRTHDAY: MARCH 8, 1996
DATE RELEASED: MAY 11, 1997
DATE RETIRED: JULY 12, 1997
STYLE # 4171
HANG TAG GENERATION: 4
ESTIMATED VALUE: $40–$50

Doodle was a short-lived Beanie, due to a trademark conflict with a fast-food chain whose mascot is a rooster named—you guessed it—Doodles. The Beanie rumor mill predicted this conflict, and collectors rushed to purchase Doodle while they could. Within just a couple months of his release, Doodle was renamed Strut, but, unlike Tabasco/Snort and Sparky/Dotty, Strut wasn't redesigned. Again, a short release time may prove to be a boon to collectors who were lucky enough to pick up Doodle before his retirement. They are predicting a significant increase in his value over time.

Dotty
(the Dalmatian)

The Beanies all thought
it was a big joke
While writing her tag,
their ink pen broke
She got in the way, and
got all spotty
So now the Beanies call
her Dotty!

BIRTHDAY: OCTOBER 17, 1996
DATE RELEASED: MAY 11, 1997
DATE RETIRED: (CURRENT)
STYLE # 4100
HANG TAG GENERATION: 4–5
ESTIMATED VALUE: $5–$7

Dotty's arrival on the Beanie scene was noted early, with collectors "spotting" her tush tag on Sparky the Dalmatian. (Sparky was retired due to a trademark conflict with the National Fire Protection Association.) Dotty, who sports black ears and a black tail, can be distinguished at a distance from the retired Sparky, whose tail and ears are white. As one of the popular group of dog Beanies, Dotty runs off retail shelves quickly and can be hard to find. In an odd reversal, recently Dotty has been found with Sparky tags! Not surprisingly, Dotty and Sparky share a style number.

Ears
(the brown rabbit)

He's been eating carrots
so long
Didn't understand what
was wrong
Couldn't see the board
during classes
Until the doctor gave him
glasses!

BIRTHDAY: APRIL 18, 1995
DATE RELEASED: JANUARY 7, 1996
DATE RETIRED: MAY 1, 1998
STYLE # 4018
HANG TAG GENERATION: 3–5
ESTIMATED VALUE: $12–$15

The oldest of the four Beanie Baby bunnies, Ears is the only rabbit
made in the lay down–style. While the pastel Floppity, Hippity, and
Hoppity are stylized and tend to be more popular among girls than
boys, Ears is designed more realistically. His rich brown plush and
long ears make him very inviting. Some collectors have reported
darker plush and a slightly larger head on fifth-generation versions,
but it's likely this is just a difference in production runs rather than
a redesign. Ears was retired with the rest of the bunnies in May
1998.

Echo
(the dolphin)

Echo the dolphin lives in the sea
Playing with her friends, like you and me
Through the waves she echoes the sound
"I'm so glad to have you around!"

BIRTHDAY: DECEMBER 21, 1996
DATE RELEASED: MAY 11, 1997
DATE RETIRED: MAY 1, 1998
STYLE # 4180
HANG TAG GENERATION: 4–5
ESTIMATED VALUE: $12–$15

When first released to replace the retiring Flash the dolphin and Splash the whale, Waves the new whale and Echo caused a lot of confusion with an identity crisis of their own. The first productions of Echo and Waves had reversed hang and tush tags! It was months before word finally got around about the mix-up. Until then, Echo was called Waves by many collectors. Finally, the tags were switched and Echo gained her true identity. Now that Echo has retired, the mistagged version will gain strength on the secondary market. Given her moderately short life as a current, even correctly tagged Echoes should do well.

Erin
(the bear)

Named after the
beautiful Emerald Isle
This Beanie Baby will
make you smile,
A bit of luck, a pot of
gold,
Light up the faces, both
young and old!

BIRTHDAY: MARCH 17, 1997
DATE RELEASED: JANUARY 31, 1998
DATE RETIRED: (CURRENT)
STYLE # 4186
HANG TAG GENERATION: 5
ESTIMATED VALUE: $5–$7

The original "colored" bears were retired in early 1996, but Erin and Princess seem to foretell the next wave. Erin, like Princess, was introduced in an announcement separate from the release of a retirement or new set of Beanies, and she was a complete surprise to collectors. Her bright green color and embroidered white shamrock make her a standout in the Beanie crowd. Originally released in limited production, her price started out quite high. As she becomes more available, her value is likely to level out. Protect yourself against counterfeits by buying only through a Ty retailer!

Flash
(the dolphin)

You know dolphins are
the smartest breed
Well Flash the dolphin
knows how to read
She's teaching her friend
Splash to read too
So maybe one day they
can both read to you.

BIRTHDAY: MAY 13, 1993
DATE RELEASED: JANUARY 8, 1994
DATE RETIRED: MAY 11, 1997
STYLE # 4021
HANG TAG GENERATION: 1–4
ESTIMATED VALUE: $100–$125

Flash and her pal, Splash the whale, were the first two of the original nine Beanies to be retired. It is easy to confuse Flash with Manny the manatee, who was retired at the same time. Collectors can tell them apart easily by looking at their bellies: Flash has a white belly, while Manny's is gray. Flash has also been reported with a different poem that reads: "You know dolphins are a smart breed/Our friend Flash knows how to read/Splash the whale is the one who taught her/Although reading is difficult under the water!"

Fleece
(the lamb)

Fleece would like to sing
a lullaby
But please be patient,
she's rather shy
When you sleep, keep
her by your ear
Her song will leave you
nothing to fear.

BIRTHDAY: MARCH 21, 1996
DATE RELEASED: JANUARY 1, 1997
DATE RETIRED: (CURRENT)
STYLE # 4125
HANG TAG GENERATION: 4–5
ESTIMATED VALUE: $5–$7

When Chops the lamb was retired, Fleece stepped in to take her place. Unlike Chops, who was ivory-colored with a black face, Fleece's fleece and face are white as snow. Fleece was the third of the five Beanies to feature "napped" fur rather than the usual plush. Though she's often thought of as an Easter Beanie (like the Beanie bunnies), she also fits right in with the rest of the farm Beanies. As a current, Fleece is still affordable and easy to find.

Flip
(the white cat)

Flip the cat is an acrobat
She loves playing on her mat
This cat flips with such grace and flair
She can somersault in mid-air!

BIRTHDAY: FEBRUARY 28, 1995
DATE RELEASED: JANUARY 7, 1996
DATE RETIRED: OCTOBER 1, 1997
STYLE # 4012
HANG TAG GENERATION: 3–4
ESTIMATED VALUE: $30–$40

As with all the white Beanies, keeping Flip clean can be a problem—especially because it's hard to resist cuddling this little kitty. Flip shares her style number with another all-white Beanie, Chilly the polar bear. Flip became very hard to find just before she was retired in October 1997, so many people did not have the opportunity to add her to their collections. As a result, desperate collectors paid a premium for her as a new retired. Since that time, her price has dropped a bit, making her a good choice for a future investment.

Floppity
(the lilac bunny)

Floppity hops from here
to there
Searching for eggs
without a care
Lavender coat from head
to toe
All dressed up and
nowhere to go!

BIRTHDAY: MAY 28, 1996
DATE RELEASED: JANUARY 1, 1997
DATE RETIRED: MAY 1, 1998
STYLE # 4118
HANG TAG GENERATION: 4–5
ESTIMATED VALUE: $12–$15

Floppity is one-third of the pastel bunny trio that was released in January 1997. After their second Easter holiday as current Beanies, speculation ran strong that Floppity, Hippity, and Hoppity would retire to make way for a new set of pastel bunnies. Sure enough, all three bunnies were among the May 1998 retirees. If you have a fifth-generation Floppity, look in the yellow star on the front of the hang tag to see if "original" is spelled "origiinal," and check the back to see if "surface" is spelled "suface." Lucky collectors may even have one of the rare tags that has a sticker over "suface" to correct the misspelling!

Flutter
(the butterfly)

(No poem)

BIRTHDAY: (NONE)
DATE RELEASED: JUNE 3, 1995
DATE RETIRED: JUNE 15, 1996
STYLE # 4043
HANG TAG GENERATION: 3
ESTIMATED VALUE: $900–$1,100

Each Flutter is unique because of her tie-dyed plush. Only her little black eyes and black string antennae show the difference between her front and back. It's too bad Flutter was retired before poems were introduced, because her grace and beautiful tie-dyed plush certainly would have inspired a wonderful poem. Flutter is a highly desirable Beanie; unfortunately, her sky-high price puts her out of range for many collectors.

Freckles
(the leopard)

From the trees he hunts
his prey
In the night and in the
day
He's the king of
camouflage
Look real close, he's no
mirage!

BIRTHDAY: JUNE 3, 1996
DATE RELEASED: JUNE 15, 1996
DATE RETIRED: (CURRENT)
STYLE # 4066
HANG TAG GENERATION: 4–5
ESTIMATED VALUE: $5–$7

Some of the fourth-generation Freckles were shipped with a hang tag that erroneously listed his birthday as July 28, 1996, instead of his true birthday, June 3, 1996. The tag with the July birthday sometimes commands a small price premium among collectors who like "oddball" Beanies. Freckles is still current, so now is a good time for collectors to add him to their assortment of Beanie Babies.

Garcia
(the bear)

**The Beanies use to
follow him around
Because Garcia traveled
from town to town
He's pretty popular as
you can see
Some even say he's
legendary.**

BIRTHDAY: AUGUST 1, 1995
DATE RELEASED: JANUARY 7, 1996
DATE RETIRED: MAY 11, 1997
STYLE # 4051
HANG TAG GENERATION: 3–4
ESTIMATED VALUE: $175–$200

Garcia, who shares a style number with the teal Teddies, was named for the late Jerry Garcia, lead singer for the popular band, Grateful Dead. Garcia's birthday takes the month and day from Jerry's own birthday, and the year from the year of his death. Garcia may have been retired due to conflicts stemming from the settling of the late singer's estate. There's a grammatical error in Garcia's poem (*use* instead of *used*), but this minor flaw has not affected his worth in any way. Garcia has been and remains one of the most popular Beanies.

Gobbles
(the turkey)

Gobbles the turkey loves
to eat
Once a year she has a
feast
I have a secret I'd like to
divulge
If she eats too much her
tummy will bulge!

BIRTHDAY: NOVEMBER 27, 1996
DATE RELEASED: OCTOBER 1, 1997
DATE RETIRED: (CURRENT)
STYLE # 4023
HANG TAG GENERATION: 4–5
ESTIMATED VALUE: $5–$7

Gobbles started her life as the most difficult to find of the five holiday-release Beanie Babies from October 1997. Since then, she has become a bit more accessible. Pre-release pictures of this Thanksgiving Beanie didn't do her justice. When she finally showed up in stores, collectors loved fanning out her tail to show her in all her glory. Collectors should buy this Beanie before she's retired.

Goldie
(the goldfish)

She's got rhythm, she's got soul
What more to like in a fish bowl?
Through sound waves Goldie swam
Because this goldfish likes to jam!

BIRTHDAY: NOVEMBER 14, 1994
DATE RELEASED: JUNE 25, 1994
DATE RETIRED: DECEMBER 31, 1997
STYLE # 4023
HANG TAG GENERATION: 1–4
ESTIMATED VALUE: $35–$45

Goldie was the first of the Beanie fish trio to be released and the last to be retired. Her bright orange plush really makes her look like a goldfish! Despite Goldie's long reign as a current, she's been fairly difficult to find since her retirement—and her price has gone up accordingly. The matching Teenie Beanie counterpart also helps to drive up Goldie's price on the secondary market.
Teenie Beanie (first set)

Gracie

(the swan)

As a duckling, she was
confused,
Birds on the lake were
quite amused.
Poking fun until she
would cry,
Now the most beautiful
swan at Ty!

BIRTHDAY: JUNE 17, 1996
DATE RELEASED: JANUARY 1, 1997
DATE RETIRED: MAY 1, 1998
STYLE # 4126
HANG TAG GENERATION: 4–5
ESTIMATED VALUE: $12–$15

Just as her poem implies, when Gracie was first released, collectors thought she was too plain to be a graceful swan. But time has served Gracie well, and she's become more popular, especially with girls. A September 13, 1998, special promotion by Ty and the Chicago Cubs links Gracie with Cubs' first baseman Mark Grace. Expect the promotional Gracie to be a home run on the secondary market, especially since she was retired prior to the game.

Grunt
(the razorback)

Some Beanies think
Grunt is tough
No surprise, he's scary
enough
But if you take him
home you'll see
Grunt is the sweetest
Beanie Baby!

BIRTHDAY: JULY 19, 1995
DATE RELEASED: JANUARY 7, 1996
DATE RETIRED: MAY 11, 1997
STYLE # 4092
HANG TAG GENERATION: 3–4
ESTIMATED VALUE: $150–$175

Grunt found popularity among boys because of his rough-and-tough image. But Grunt also has a built-in fan-following consisting of fans of the University of Arkansas Razorbacks! Collectors who are considering buying this Beanie should make sure to check the felt spikes along his back, as the felt may show signs of wear long before the plush does. Grunt, whose price started to increase a few months after his retirement, remains one of the more expensive of the May 1997 retirees. Be wary of "wrinkled" Grunts. They may be counterfeit.

Happy
(the hippo)

Happy the Hippo loves to wade
In the river and in the shade
When Happy shoots water out of his snout
You'll know he's happy without a doubt!

(gray)	*(lavender)*
BIRTHDAY: FEBRUARY 25, 1994	BIRTHDAY: FEBRUARY 25, 1994
DATE RELEASED: JUNE 25, 1994	DATE RELEASED: JUNE 3, 1995
DATE RETIRED: JUNE 3, 1995	DATE RETIRED: MAY 1, 1998
STYLE # 4061	STYLE # 4061
HANG TAG GENERATION: 1–3	HANG TAG GENERATION: 3–5
ESTIMATED VALUE: $750–$850	ESTIMATED VALUE: $15–$20

Originally released with gray plush, Happy was changed to lavender in mid-1995. Ty may have thought that a gray hippo wasn't fanciful enough for the children for whom Beanies are intended. With his long lifespan, Happy had lost favor for a while—until it was discovered that he was going to be released as part of the second McDonald's Teenie Beanie collection! Add to this his desirability as a May 1998 retiree, and Happy should be a good bet on the secondary market.
Teenie Beanie (second set)

Hippity
(the mint bunny)

Hippity is a cute little bunny
Dressed in green, he looks quite funny
Twitching his nose in the air
Sniffing a flower here and there!

BIRTHDAY: JUNE 1, 1996
DATE RELEASED: JANUARY 1, 1997
DATE RETIRED: MAY 1, 1998
STYLE # 4119
HANG TAG GENERATION: 4–5
ESTIMATED VALUE: $12–$15

This "cool" mint bunny has long floppy ears like his two pastel bunny buddies, Floppity and Hoppity. In the summer and early fall of 1997, Hippity was the most difficult of the trio to find. All the bunnies were in demand for the Easter holiday, amidst rumors they would be retired. Sure enough, they were retired shortly after Easter. The early-fifth-generation Hippitys have the same tag typos as Floppity, Hoppity, Blackie, Curly, Peace, and Valentino, with the double-i "origiinal" and missing-r "suface." More-recent Hippitys can be found with a sticker with the correct spelling covering the "suface" misspelling, so check those tags!

Hissy
(the snake)

Curled and coiled and
ready to play,
He waits for you
patiently every day
He'll keep his best
friend, but not his skin
And stay with you
through thick and thin!

BIRTHDAY: APRIL 4, 1997
DATE RELEASED: DECEMBER 31, 1998
DATE RETIRED: (CURRENT)
STYLE # 4185
HANG TAG GENERATION: 5
ESTIMATED VALUE: $5–$7

Hissy is a coveted Beanie for many collectors, who love his coiled
shape. This long-awaited replacement for the retired Slither isn't
quite as long as his serpentine friend when he's stretched out, but
he's long enough to be the second-longest Beanie. There's still time
to snap Slither up, as he remains a current and is affordable and
fairly easy to find.

Hoot
(the owl)

Late to bed, late to rise
Nevertheless, Hoot's
quite wise
Studies by candlelight,
nothing new
Like a president, do you
know Whooo?

BIRTHDAY: AUGUST 9, 1995
DATE RELEASED: JANUARY 7, 1996
DATE RETIRED: OCTOBER 1, 1997
STYLE # 4073
HANG TAG GENERATION: 3–4
ESTIMATED VALUE: $40–$50

This tiny owl is one of the shortest Beanies made and can fit in even
a small child's hand. Check out the poem on fourth-generation
Hoots to see if the word "quite" is misspelled "qutie." Though not as
rare as some other tag errors, this mistake does make Hoot more
valuable. Since his retirement in October 1997, this retiree's value
has started to climb, but Hoot is still inexpensive enough to add to
almost any collection.

Hoppity
(the rose bunny)

Hopscotch is what she
likes to play
If you don't join in,
she'll hop away
So play a game if you
have the time,
She likes to play, rain or
shine!

BIRTHDAY: APRIL 3, 1996
DATE RELEASED: JANUARY 1, 1997
DATE RETIRED: MAY 1, 1998
STYLE # 4117
HANG TAG GENERATION: 4–5
ESTIMATED VALUE: $12–$15

Possibly the most popular of the three pastel bunnies, this little rose-colored bunny has been in great demand. Though Hippity was hard to find for a while in 1997, at the start of the 1998 Easter holiday Hoppity seemed to be the bunny in hiding. With her retirement, the secondary market may be flooded with rose bunnies at first, and her price may take a small dip as a result, but it will increase as she becomes scarcer again. As on the other pastel bunnies, the fifth-generation tag misspells the word "original" as "origiinal," and "surface" is spelled without the "r" on the back. Lucky collectors might find one of the rare Hoppitys with the sticker that corrects the "suface" error.

Humphrey
(the camel)

(No poem)

BIRTHDAY: (NONE)
DATE RELEASED: JUNE 25, 1994
DATE RETIRED: JUNE 15, 1995
STYLE # 4060
HANG TAG GENERATION: 1–3
ESTIMATED VALUE: $1,800–$2,000

Who could resist this dromedary who can't even stand on his own four legs? Humphrey's forlorn expression and floppy legs make him a prized member of any Beanie collection. Humphrey was retired early in Beanie history and is difficult to find in mint condition with his tag. His retired pricing reflects it, but there are still many people who long to have a Beanie classic like Humphrey—with or without his hang tag.

Iggy

(the iguana)

Sitting on a rock,
basking in the sun
Is this Iguana's idea of
fun
Towel and glasses, book
and beach chair
His life is so perfect
without a care!

BIRTHDAY: AUGUST 12, 1997
DATE RELEASED: DECEMBER 31, 1997
DATE RETIRED: (CURRENT)
STYLE # 4038
HANG TAG GENERATION: 5
ESTIMATED VALUE: $5–$7

Tie-dyed blue Iggy and his cohort, the colorful Rainbow the chameleon, have raised a lot of controversy. The first shipments of Iggy and Rainbow seemed to have switched tags like Echo the dolphin and Waves the whale, but it may be that it was actually their fabric that got switched and not the tags. Iggy's body is shaped more like a chameleon, and Rainbow's body shape is more like that of an iguana. Sightings of a retagged Iggy (and Rainbow) have been reported, but the value of the mistagged versions remains to be determined.

Inch
(the inchworm)

Inch the worm is a friend of mine
He goes so slow all the time
Inching around from here to there
Traveling the world without a care!

(felt antennae)	*(yarn antennae)*
BIRTHDAY: SEPTEMBER 3, 1995	BIRTHDAY: SEPTEMBER 3, 1995
DATE RELEASED: JUNE 3, 1995	DATE RELEASED: OCTOBER 15, 1996
DATE RETIRED: OCTOBER 15, 1996	DATE RETIRED: MAY 1, 1998
STYLE # 4044	STYLE # 4044
HANG TAG GENERATION: 3–4	HANG TAG GENERATION: 4–5
ESTIMATED VALUE: $175–$200	ESTIMATED VALUE: $12–$15

Rainbow-colored segments and a wavy body make Inch look as if he may actually wiggle his way along. Inch was originally introduced with felt antennae instead of the current yarn, but the felt didn't wear well (just like Lizzy's and Slither's tongues). The recently retired Inch is one of the second batch of McDonald's Teenie Beanies (released in May 1998), so grab him now, before his price skyrockets.
Teenie Beanie (second set)

Inky
(the octopus)

Inky's head is big and
round
As he swims he makes
no sound
If you need a hand,
don't hesitate
Inky can help because
he has eight!

(no mouth)
BIRTHDAY: NOVEMBER 29, 1994
DATE RELEASED: JUNE 25, 1994
DATE RETIRED: SEPTEMBER 12, 1994
STYLE # 4028
HANG TAG GENERATION: 1–2
ESTIMATED VALUE: $800–$950

(with mouth)
BIRTHDAY: NOVEMBER 29, 1994
DATE RELEASED: SEPT. 12, 1994
DATE RETIRED: JUNE 3, 1995
STYLE # 4028
HANG TAG GENERATION: 3
ESTIMATED VALUE: $650–$750

(pink)
BIRTHDAY: NOVEMBER 29, 1994
DATE RELEASED: JUNE 3, 1995
DATE RETIRED: MAY 1, 1998
STYLE # 4028
HANG TAG GENERATION: 3–5
ESTIMATED VALUE: $25–$35

Inky was originally released in a taupe color with no mouth. (This may be because an octopus's mouth isn't under his eyes, it's under his head.) The no-mouth Inky was out less than three months before Ty added a V-shaped mouth under his eyes. Ty turned him pink just nine months later. Another oddity is that Inky can be found with seven or nine legs instead of the usual eight.

Jolly
(the walrus)

Jolly the walrus is not very serious
He laughs and laughs until he's delirious
He often reminds me of my dad
Always happy, never sad!

BIRTHDAY: DECEMBER 2, 1996
DATE RELEASED: MAY 11, 1997
DATE RETIRED: MAY 1, 1998
STYLE # 4082
HANG TAG GENERATION: 4–5
ESTIMATED VALUE: $12–$15

Jolly was a welcome replacement for Tusk the walrus, who was retired in January 1997. Some collectors had considered Tusk boring. Though Jolly shared the same basic body shape with Echo the dolphin and Waves the whale, his mustache won him immediate favor. The long, soft fuzz makes Jolly unusual, which might be why he was tough to find in stores before his retirement. Collectors may have to do some serious hunting to locate him. Values should be strong based on his rather short stint as a current.

Kiwi
(the toucan)

Kiwi waits for April
showers
Watching a garden
bloom with flowers
There trees grow with
fruit that's sweet
I'm sure you'll guess his
favorite treat!

BIRTHDAY: SEPTEMBER 16, 1995
DATE RELEASED: JUNE 3, 1995
DATE RETIRED: JANUARY 1, 1997
STYLE # 4070
HANG TAG GENERATION: 3–4
ESTIMATED VALUE: $160–$190

Kiwi is one confused Beanie! Kiwi fruit and kiwi birds are both indigenous to New Zealand; but toucans are native to Central and South America. This Beanie bird was released at the same time as his body double, Caw the crow, and was retired in January 1997. Since then, Kiwi's colorful beak and tail have gained great popularity. Check all third-generation Kiwi hang tags for his name in all lowercase letters; this variation might make him a little more valuable.

Lefty
(the donkey)

Donkeys to the left,
elephants to the right
Often seems like a crazy
sight
This whole game seems
very funny
Until you realize they're
spending
Your money!

BIRTHDAY: JULY 4, 1996
DATE RELEASED: JUNE 15, 1996
DATE RETIRED: JANUARY 1, 1997
STYLE # 4086
HANG TAG GENERATION: 4
ESTIMATED VALUE: $250–$300

Patriotic Beanies Lefty, Righty the elephant, and Libearty the bear were among the first to be released with a fourth-generation hang tag, some of which have "surface" spelled "sufrace" on the backs. All three Beanies were retired within six months of their announcements, making them some of the shortest-lived Beanies and the most valuable of the January 1997 retirees. Lefty and his Republican counterpart were released to commemorate the 1996 presidential election. As with all the patriotic Beanies, it's possible to find this little donkey without a flag or with an upside-down flag, two rare errors that greatly increase Lefty's value.

Legs
(the frog)

Legs lives in a hollow
log
Legs likes to play leap
frog
If you like to hang out at
the lake
Legs will be the new
friend you'll make!

BIRTHDAY: APRIL 25, 1993
DATE RELEASED: JANUARY 8, 1994
DATE RETIRED: OCTOBER 1, 1997
STYLE # 4020
HANG TAG GENERATION: 1–4
ESTIMATED VALUE: $20–$25

It's not easy being green. Poor little Legs was much maligned for being too plain, but as one of the original nine Beanies, he will always have a place in Beanie history. Even though he was retired relatively early (October 1997), Legs had been around long enough for most collectors to pick him up. This kept his price low, however, and his value has nowhere to go but up. You can still pick up this original at a very reasonable price, and that might be a pretty smart move.

Libearty
(the bear)

I am called Libearty
I wear the flag for all to
see
Hope and freedom is my
way
That's why I wear flag
USA

BIRTHDAY: SUMMER 1996
DATE RELEASED: JUNE 15, 1996
DATE RETIRED: JANUARY 1, 1997
STYLE # 4057
HANG TAG GENERATION: 4
ESTIMATED VALUE: $325–$375

Released to honor the 1996 Summer Olympics in Atlanta, Libearty had to relinquish the word "Olympics" from her tag because the International Olympic Committee would not give Ty permission to use it. Despite some people believing that the error is rare, Libeartys that have the word "Beanie" spelled "Beanine" are actually more common and slightly less valuable than correct Libeartys. Clear tag connectors and whited-out or cut-off website information are also common. Libearty is the most popular of the American Trio and has increased in value even more quickly than the other two members, Lefty the donkey and Righty the elephant.

Lizzy
(the lizard)

Her best friend Legs was
at her house waiting
Today is the day they go
roller blading
But Lizzy Lou had to
stay home
So Legs had to roller
blade alone.

(tie-dyed)	**(blue)**
BIRTHDAY: MAY 11, 1995	BIRTHDAY: MAY 11, 1995
DATE RELEASED: JUNE 3, 1995	DATE RELEASED: JANUARY 7, 1996
DATE RETIRED: JANUARY 7, 1996	DATE RETIRED: DECEMBER 31, 1997
STYLE # 4033	STYLE # 4033
HANG TAG GENERATION: 3	HANG TAG GENERATION: 3–4
ESTIMATED VALUE: $900–$1,100	ESTIMATED VALUE: $20–$25

Once Legs the frog was retired, it was clear Lizzy wouldn't be far behind. Technically, Lizzy retired before fifth-generation hang tags came out, but she can be found sporting one. The original Lizzy featured tie-dyed plush, but she was redesigned with the current black-and-blue plush. The redesigned Lizzy was one of the original McDonald's Teenie Beanies, although the Teenie version is named Lizz. Lizzy also can be found with another version of her poem: "Lizzy loves Legs the frog/She hides with him under logs/Both of them search for flies/Underneath the clear blue skies!" This little lizard is still inexpensive enough for almost any collector to obtain.
Teenie Beanie (first set)

Lucky
(the ladybug)

Lucky the lady bug loves
the lotto
"Someone must win"
that's her motto
But save your dimes and
even a penny
Don't spend on the lotto
and
You'll have many!

(seven felt spots)
BIRTHDAY: MAY 1, 1995
DATE RELEASED: JUNE 25, 1994
DATE RETIRED: FEBRUARY 27, 1996
STYLE # 4040
HANG TAG GENERATION: 1–3
ESTIMATED VALUE: $200–$225

(21 printed spots)
BIRTHDAY: MAY 1, 1995
DATE RELEASED: JUNE 15, 1996
DATE RETIRED: (UNKNOWN)
STYLE # 4040
HANG TAG GENERATION: 4
ESTIMATED VALUE: $550–$650

(11 printed spots)
BIRTHDAY: MAY 1, 1995
DATE RELEASED: SEPT. 15, 1996 (APPROXIMATE)
DATE RETIRED: MAY 1, 1998
STYLE # 4040
HANG TAG GENERATION: 4–5
ESTIMATED VALUE: $20–$25

Lucky first came out with seven felt spots glued onto her back, but, after almost two years, Ty switched the fabric to printed spots. Many of the seven-spot Luckys have become six- to zero-spot Luckys over time as the glued-on spots have fallen off. But the rarest of the Lucky variations is the 21-spot Lucky, whose smaller spots were printed onto the fabric.

Magic
(the dragon)

Magic the Dragon lives
in a dream
The most beautiful that
you have ever seen
Through magic lands she
likes to fly
Look up and watch her,
way up high!

BIRTHDAY: JUNE 8, 1995
DATE RELEASED: JUNE 3, 1995
DATE RETIRED: DECEMBER 31, 1997
STYLE # 4088
HANG TAG GENERATION: 3–4
ESTIMATED VALUE: $40–$50

The only certain thing about Magic's variations is that there's nothing certain about them! The oldest versions have pale pink thread used in the stitching of her wings and nostrils, while slightly later versions use hot pink thread. The latest version can be found with both colors, and nobody seems to know which is more common. Also, the third-generation Magics usually have puffier wings than other versions. Pick up this beautiful dragon now before her price takes wing!

Manny
(the manatee)

Manny is sometimes
called a sea cow
She likes to twirl and like
to bow
Manny sure is glad you
bought her
Because it's so lonely
under water!

BIRTHDAY: JUNE 8, 1995
DATE RELEASED: JANUARY 7, 1996
DATE RETIRED: MAY 11, 1997
STYLE # 4081
HANG TAG GENERATION: 3–4
ESTIMATED VALUE: $150–$175

The all-gray Manny is often confused with the white-bellied Flash the dolphin, especially as they were retired at the same time. But Manny was not as popular as Flash was as a current, nor was she available as long as Flash was. As a result of her endangerment, her retired price has gone up faster than Flash's price. A mint-condition Manny is still a good investment, especially if she sports a rare third-generation hang tag. A grammatical error in Manny's tag (*like* instead of *likes*) doesn't affect this Beanie's value. Be wary of counterfeit Mannys coming into the secondary market.

Maple
(the bear)

Maple the bear likes to
ski
With his friends, he plays
hockey.
He loves his pancakes
and eats every crumb,
Can you guess which
country he's from?

BIRTHDAY: JULY 1, 1996
DATE RELEASED: JANUARY 1, 1997
DATE RETIRED: (CURRENT)
STYLE # 4600
HANG TAG GENERATION: 4–5
ESTIMATED VALUE: $7–$15

Released to commemorate Canadian Independence Day and available for retail sale only in Canada, Maple's original name was Pride. About 3,000 to 5,000 Beanie Babies were produced and released with a Pride tush tag. This original version is almost impossible to find, and the current Maple isn't much easier to find, even in Canada. A special version of Maple was made available in limited edition during the last week of August 1997 to help benefit the Special Olympics. Being Canadian, all Maples have a second tush tag in both French and English. Buy carefully! There are counterfeits around.

Mel
(the koala)

**How do you name a
Koala bear?
It's rather tough, I do
declare!
It confuses me, I get into
a funk
I'll name him Mel, after
my favorite hunk!**

BIRTHDAY: JANUARY 15, 1996
DATE RELEASED: JANUARY 1, 1997
DATE RETIRED: (CURRENT)
STYLE # 4162
HANG TAG GENERATION: 4–5
ESTIMATED VALUE: $5–$7

When is a bear not really a bear? When it's a Koala! Mel, like his
Australian pal, Pouch the kangaroo, is really a marsupial. There
have been lots of rumors about Mel being retired because of the
reference in his tag poem to actor "hunk" Mel Gibson, but after two
years of Beaniehood, Mel seems to be safe from trademark woes.
It's important to note that Teenie Mel, in the second set of McDonald's Teenie Beanies, will mean added value for Mel in his retirement years.
Teenie Beanie (second set)

Mystic
(the unicorn)

Once upon a time so
far away
A unicorn was born
one day in May
Keep Mystic with you,
she's a prize
You'll see the magic
in her blue eyes!

(fine mane)
BIRTHDAY: MAY 21, 1994
DATE RELEASED: JUNE 25, 1994
DATE RETIRED: (UNKNOWN)
STYLE # 4007
HANG TAG GENERATION: 1–3
ESTIMATED VALUE: $225–$275

(coarse mane)
BIRTHDAY: MAY 21, 1994
DATE RELEASED: (UNKNOWN)
DATE RETIRED: OCTOBER 23, 1997
STYLE # 4007
HANG TAG GENERATION: 3–4
ESTIMATED VALUE: $30–$40

(iridescent horn)
BIRTHDAY: MAY 21, 1994
DATE RELEASED: OCTOBER 23, 1997
DATE RETIRED: (CURRENT)
STYLE # 4007
HANG TAG GENERATION: 4–5
ESTIMATED VALUE: $5–$7

Mystic's mane and tail were originally made of thinner white yarn
than that of the current version. Sometime along the way, the fine
yarn gave way to coarser yarn. Rumors of a Mystic with a horn
made from the same material as Magic the dragon's wings
abounded before two such Mystics were found in stores in summer
1997. Those Beanies were a prototype for the iridescent-horned
Mystic that was released in October 1997.

95

Nanook
(the Husky)

Nanook is a dog that
loves cold weather
To him a sled is light as
a feather
Over the snow and
through the slush
He runs at hearing the
cry of "mush"!

BIRTHDAY: NOVEMBER 21, 1996
DATE RELEASED: MAY 11, 1997
DATE RETIRED: (CURRENT)
STYLE # 4104
HANG TAG GENERATION: 4–5
ESTIMATED VALUE: $5–$7

Collectors take one look at Nanook's big blue eyes and become
hooked. This little Husky is certainly one of the most popular of the
dog Beanies, and he still can be tough to find in stores. Despite his
warm and fuzzy good looks and the fact many people love him,
Nanook is not more valuable than any of the other Beanie dogs at
this point, especially due to his status as a current.

Nip
(the gold cat)

His name is Nipper, but
we call him Nip
His best friend is a black
cat named Zip
Nip likes to run in races
for fun
He runs so fast he's
always number one!

(white face and belly)
BIRTHDAY: MARCH 6, 1994
DATE RELEASED: JANUARY 7, 1995
DATE RETIRED: JANUARY 7, 1996
STYLE # 4003
HANG TAG GENERATION: 2–3
ESTIMATED VALUE: $500–$600

(all gold)
BIRTHDAY: MARCH 6, 1994
DATE RELEASED: JANUARY 7, 1996
DATE RETIRED: MARCH 10, 1996
STYLE # 4003
HANG TAG GENERATION: 3
ESTIMATED VALUE: $850–$950

(white paws)
BIRTHDAY: MARCH 6, 1994
DATE RELEASED: MARCH 10, 1996
DATE RETIRED: DECEMBER 31, 1997
STYLE # 4003
HANG TAG GENERATION: 3–4
ESTIMATED VALUE: $20–$25

The first version of Nip had a big, rounded head, white muzzle,
white belly, and pink ears and whiskers. The second version (the
rarest and most valuable) was all gold with pink ears. The last, and
most widely available, Nip had white ears, paws, and whiskers. This
kitty was retired before the fifth-generation tags came out, but
nonetheless a few lucky collectors have found a fifth-generation Nip.

Nuts
(the squirrel)

With his bushy tail, he'll
scamper up a tree
The most cheerful critter
you'll ever see,
He's nuts about nuts,
and he loves to chat,
Have you ever seen a
squirrel like that?

BIRTHDAY: JANUARY 21, 1996
DATE RELEASED: JANUARY 1, 1997
DATE RETIRED: (CURRENT)
STYLE # 4114
HANG TAG GENERATION: 4–5
ESTIMATED VALUE: $5–$7

Nuts has the coolest tail of any of the Beanies: soft, full, and fluffy. Despite this appealing characteristic, and the fact Nuts is the only Beanie squirrel Ty has issued, there's nothing special about Nuts to lend him extra value on the secondary market. Collectors should make sure to purchase him in stores for face value and squirrel him away before he's retired and his price goes up accordingly.

Patti
(the platypus)

Ran into Patti one day
while walking
Believe me she wouldn't
stop talking
Listened and listened to
her speak
That would explain her
extra large beak!

**(raspberry, magenta, and
deep fuchsia)**
BIRTHDAY: JANUARY 6, 1993
DATE RELEASED: JANUARY 8, 1994
DATE RETIRED: FEBRUARY 28, 1995
STYLE # 4025
HANG TAG GENERATION: 1–3
ESTIMATED VALUE: $700–$1,000

(fuchsia)
BIRTHDAY: JANUARY 6, 1993
DATE RELEASED: FEB. 28, 1995
DATE RETIRED: MAY 1, 1998
STYLE # 4025
HANG TAG GENERATION: 3–5
ESTIMATED VALUE: $15–$20

Patti is one of the original nine Beanies, but she's undergone several color changes. Officially Patti has had only two colors, but it could be considered four. The first Patti, released before the original nine Beanies, is a deep fuchsia color with first-generation hang tag and four-line black-and-white tush tag. The second and third versions are often referred to as raspberry and magenta. The last version is a lighter fuchsia. If you're not sure what version yours is, hold her up next to Inch the inchworm's tail. The last version matches Inch exactly. Look for Teenie Patti, too, in the first set of McDonald's Teenie Beanies!
Teenie Beanie (first set)

Peace
(the bear)

All races, all colors,
under the sun
Join hands together and
have some fun
Dance to the music, rock
and roll is the sound
Symbols of peace and
love abound!

BIRTHDAY: FEBRUARY 1, 1996
DATE RELEASED: MAY 11, 1997
DATE RETIRED: (CURRENT)
STYLE # 4053
HANG TAG GENERATION: 4–5
ESTIMATED VALUE: $5–$7

Still unbelievably popular more than a year after his official release,
tie-dyed Peace is one of the hardest current Beanies to find in stores
due to his being the last of the May 1997 newbeans to be shipped.
Decked out just like Garcia the bear, Peace sports a multicolored
peace symbol embroidered on his chest. Brightly colored versions
have been more sought after than those with pale-colored tie-dye
patterns. Fifth-generation Peace has been shipped with the "origiinal" and "suface" misspellings on his tag. Peace only comes with
the new Teddy face.

Peanut
(the elephant)

Peanut the elephant
walks on tip-toes
Quietly sneaking
wherever she goes
She'll sneak up on
you and a hug
You will get
Peanut is a friend
you won't soon
forget!

(royal blue)	**(light blue)**
BIRTHDAY: JANUARY 25, 1995	BIRTHDAY: JANUARY 25, 1995
DATE RELEASED: JUNE 3, 1995	DATE RELEASED: OCTOBER 2, 1995
DATE RETIRED: OCTOBER 2, 1995	DATE RETIRED: MAY 1, 1998
STYLE # 4062	STYLE # 4062
HANG TAG GENERATION: 3	HANG TAG GENERATION: 3–5
ESTIMATED VALUE: $4,500–$5,000	ESTIMATED VALUE: $12–$15

Her Majesty, the Royal Blue Peanut, is without a doubt the most sought-after Beanie. Released only for a very short period, and mainly before Beanie Babies became a national passion, Peanut's value has skyrocketed. Ironically, her beautiful deep blue plush apparently was an error and was replaced with the more common light blue color. Peanut can also be seen as part of the second McDonald's Teenie Beanie set and will find new popularity since her retirement and as collectors search for "moms" for their Teenies.
Teenie Beanie (second set)

Peking
(the panda)

(No poem)

BIRTHDAY: (NONE)
DATE RELEASED: JUNE 25, 1994
DATE RETIRED: JANUARY 7, 1996
STYLE # 4013
HANG TAG GENERATION: 1–3
ESTIMATED VALUE: $1,750–$2,250

Peking is one of the four lay down–style bears released into the Beanie Babies collection. The black circles around his eyes give him a sad air. Because he was retired before Beanies became hot, Peking is very difficult to find in mint condition, and almost impossible to find with his tags in any condition. Be wary of counterfeit Pekings that have come into the secondary market. Study him closely before you spend a lot of money to obtain this extremely rare specimen.

Pinchers
(the lobster)

This lobster loves to pinch
Eating his food inch by inch
Balancing carefully with his tail
Moving forward slow as a snail!

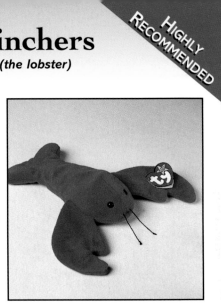

(Punchers)	**(Pinchers)**
BIRTHDAY: (NONE)	BIRTHDAY: JUNE 19, 1993
DATE RELEASED: JANUARY 8, 1994	DATE RELEASED: JANUARY 8, 1994
DATE RETIRED: (UNKNOWN)	DATE RETIRED: MAY 1, 1998
STYLE # 4026	STYLE # 4026
HANG TAG GENERATION: 1	HANG TAG GENERATION: 1–5
ESTIMATED VALUE: $4,000–$4,750	ESTIMATED VALUE: $15–$20

Pinchers, a member of the original nine Beanie Babies, was retired on May 1, 1998. Slightly redesigned from an early "Punchers" Beanie, this Pinchers's feelers were shortened slightly, and the inner two segments on his tail are closer together. Unless the hang tag reads "Punchers," this Beanie is probably just an old Pinchers. Pinchers is a member of the second McDonald's Teenie Beanie set. Due to his Teenie counterpart and his recent retired status, Pinchers should see a surge of renewed interest.
Teenie Beanie (second set)

Pinky
(the flamingo)

Pinky loves the
everglades
From the hottest pink
she's made
With floppy legs and big
orange beak
She's the Beanie that
you seek!

BIRTHDAY: FEBRUARY 13, 1995
DATE RELEASED: JUNE 3, 1995
DATE RETIRED: (CURRENT)
STYLE # 4072
HANG TAG GENERATION: 3–5
ESTIMATED VALUE: $5–$7

Even non-collectors recognize long-legged Pinky. Her bright pink color, bright orange beak, and long legs distinguish her from the crowd—any crowd. Pinky has been difficult to find in some areas of the country, thanks to her popularity as both a Beanie and a "mom" to the hardest-to-find Teenie Beanie from the original McDonald's set. She's going to be one hot flamingo when she retires, so pick her up as soon as possible.
Teenie Beanie (first set)

Pouch
(the kangaroo)

My little pouch is handy
I've found
It helps me carry my
baby around
I hop up and down
without any fear
Knowing my baby is safe
and near.

BIRTHDAY: NOVEMBER 6, 1996
DATE RELEASED: JANUARY 1, 1997
DATE RETIRED: (CURRENT)
STYLE # 4161
HANG TAG GENERATION: 4–5
ESTIMATED VALUE: $5–$7

Longtime rumors of Pouch's retirement have been greatly exaggerated. Concerns about her little joey's head coming unsewn from her pouch seem to be unfounded, but the rumors continue, and one has to wonder if maybe she will be redesigned with an entire baby (instead of just a head!), without one at all, or retired completely. She becomes more difficult to find just before any Ty announcement—probably for that very reason. But Pouch is one cute kangaroo and a great addition to any collection.

Pounce
(the cat)

Sneaking and slinking
down the hall
To pounce upon a fluffy
yarn ball
Under the tables, around
the chairs
Through the rooms and
down the stairs!

BIRTHDAY: AUGUST 28, 1997
DATE RELEASED: DECEMBER 31, 1997
DATE RETIRED: (CURRENT)
STYLE # 4122
HANG TAG GENERATION: 5
ESTIMATED VALUE: $5–$7

This cute kitty really does have all-brown tie-dyed plush. It's not a mistake, even though many thought it might have been. The tie-dyed plush makes each Pounce unique. After Pounce's initial announcement, it didn't take long for people to start wondering if the name "Pounce" might cause yet another trademark problem, this time with a cat food by the same name. Time will tell, but in the meantime, pounce on this feline Beanie just in case he does get renamed.

Prance
(the cat)

She darts around and
swats the air
Then looks confused
when nothing's there
Pick her up and pet her
soft fur
Listen closely, and you'll
hear her purr!

BIRTHDAY: NOVEMBER 20, 1997
DATE RELEASED: DECEMBER 31, 1997
DATE RETIRED: (CURRENT)
STYLE # 4123
HANG TAG GENERATION: 5
ESTIMATED VALUE: $5–$7

The tiger stripes on Prance make her a standout from all the other
Beanie cats. What a great addition to the cat collection she is!
However, her stripes can cause manufacturing errors such as the
stripes on one side being the wrong direction or her tail going the
wrong way. Prance should be a member of the Beanie line for some
time, so don't panic and pay high secondary-market prices for her
just because she's fairly new.

Princess
(the bear)

Like an angel, she came
from heaven above
She shared her
compassion, her pain,
her love
She only stayed with us
long enough to teach
The world to share, to
give, to reach.

BIRTHDAY: (NONE)
DATE RELEASED: OCTOBER 29, 1997
DATE RETIRED: (CURRENT)
STYLE # 4300
HANG TAG GENERATION: SPECIAL
ESTIMATED VALUE: $5–$7

Beautiful in every way, the deep royal purple Princess stole the
hearts of collectors immediately. She is also highly desired by
collectors of Princess Diana memorabilia. Ty announces on her
unique hang tag that all profits will be donated to Diana's memorial
fund. Many retailers followed Ty's lead and raffled or auctioned off
Princess to raise money for various charities. Don't worry about
whether Princess's tush tag says PVC or PE pellets: Even some of
the first shipments contained the new PE pellets. Just be happy to
have this English Rose in your collection.

Puffer
(the puffin)

What in the world does a
puffin do?
We're sure that you
would like to know too
We asked Puffer how she
spends her days
Before she answered,
she flew away!

BIRTHDAY: NOVEMBER 3, 1997
DATE RELEASED: DECEMBER 31, 1997
DATE RETIRED: (CURRENT)
STYLE # 4181
HANG TAG GENERATION: 5
ESTIMATED VALUE: $5–$7

Reminiscent of the retired Kiwi the toucan, Puffer features a flashy
red-and-yellow beak that makes her a bright standout in the Beanie
class of January 1998. Don't expect Puffer to fly away into retirement too quickly: Collectors can—and should—afford to wait and
find her in stores rather than pay higher prices on the secondary
market.

Pugsly
(the Pug)

Pugsly is picky about
what he will wear
Never a spot, a stain or
a tear
Image is something of
which he'll gloat
Until he noticed his
wrinkled coat!

BIRTHDAY: MAY 2, 1996
DATE RELEASED: MAY 11, 1997
DATE RETIRED: (CURRENT)
STYLE # 4106
HANG TAG GENERATION: 4–5
ESTIMATED VALUE: $5–$7

Pugsly the Pug dog is notable for his black snout and ears, his curly little tail, and his wrinkles. As a member of the popular Beanie dog family, Pugsly immediately becomes a valued member of any Beanie Baby collection. Pick Pugsly up as a current, before he hits the secondary market and his price rises accordingly.

Quackers

(the duck)

There is a duck by the
name of Quackers
Every night he eats
animal crackers
He swims in a lake that's
clear and blue
But he'll come to the
shore to be with you!

(wingless)	**(with wings)**
BIRTHDAY: APRIL 19, 1994	BIRTHDAY: APRIL 19, 1994
DATE RELEASED: JUNE 25, 1994	DATE RELEASED: JANUARY 7, 1995
DATE RETIRED: JANUARY 7, 1995	DATE RETIRED: MAY 1, 1998
STYLE # 4024	STYLE # 4024
HANG TAG GENERATION: 1–2	HANG TAG GENERATION: 2–5
ESTIMATED VALUE: $1,750–$2,250	ESTIMATED VALUE: $12–$15

The very earliest examples of this bright yellow duck were shipped
without wings. This wingless version is very rare and highly desirable, and almost impossible to find with his tag. Interestingly, some
of the second-generation tags on both the wingless and winged
versions record his name as "Quacker." Quackers's Teenie Beanie
counterpart from the first McDonald's set is named Quacks.
Collectors lucky enough to own a Quackers thought it was just
ducky when he was retired on May 1, 1998.
Teenie Beanie (first set)

Radar
(the bat)

Radar the bat flies late
at night
He can soar to an
amazing height
If you see something as
high as a star
Take a good look, it
might be Radar!

BIRTHDAY: OCTOBER 30, 1995
DATE RELEASED: SEPTEMBER 1, 1995
DATE RETIRED: MAY 11, 1997
STYLE # 4091
HANG TAG GENERATION: 3–4
ESTIMATED VALUE: $150–$175

Confusion reigned when Ty announced the retirement of both
Radar and Spooky the ghost on January 29, 1997, then retracted
the announcement the next day. Radar hung around until his
retirement that May; Spooky lasted until December 31, 1997.
Radar doesn't have the Velcro hook-and-loop fasteners on his wings
that his replacement Batty has, but he folds up very neatly when his
wings are wrapped around his body. His red eyes belie the fact that
bats don't see very well; bats do most of their navigating by a type
of—what else?—radar!

Rainbow
(the chameleon)

Red, green, blue and yellow
This chameleon is a colorful fellow
A blend of colors, his own unique hue
Rainbow was made especially for you!

BIRTHDAY: OCTOBER 14, 1997
DATE RELEASED: DECEMBER 31, 1997
DATE RETIRED: (CURRENT)
STYLE # 4037
HANG TAG GENERATION: 5
ESTIMATED VALUE: $5–$7

With his spiky back, this chameleon looks a lot like an iguana, which could be part of the reason for the confusion between him and Iggy the iguana. Rainbow was first delivered with Iggy's tag, and vice versa. But many collectors believe it was the two animals' fabric that was switched, because the tags and body styles seemed to match. The brightly tie-dyed Rainbow has been spotted with a correct tag, so anything might happen to Rainbow's value on the secondary market. If Echo the dolphin and Waves the whale are any indication, the mistags' value will be slightly higher than the correctly tagged versions'. The latest shipment of Iggys feature a short pink velveteen tongue. It's unclear if this is a permanent redesign.

Rex
(the tyrannosaurus)

(No poem)

BIRTHDAY: (NONE)
DATE RELEASED: JUNE 3, 1995
DATE RETIRED: JUNE 15, 1996
STYLE # 4086
HANG TAG GENERATION: 3
ESTIMATED VALUE: $850–$1,000

Retired before he was granted a birthday or a poem, this dinosaur's plush is tie-dyed with pink, hot pink, bright magenta, violet, blue, and even orange. Each Rex is a unique work of art. The highly sought-after tie-dyed dinosaur trio of Bronty, Rex, and Steg remains on the wish list of many collectors. Buying them on the secondary market may force collectors to break into the piggy bank, but it's doubtful they'll regret it. Beanie fans should note that Rex, once retired, donated his style number to Lefty the donkey.

Righty
(the elephant)

Donkeys to the left,
elephants to the right
Often seems like a crazy
sight
This whole game seems
very funny
Until you realize they're
spending
Your money!

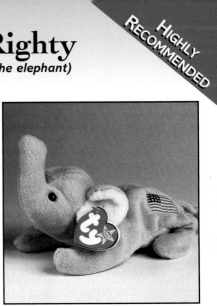

BIRTHDAY: JULY 4, 1996
DATE RELEASED: JUNE 15, 1996
DATE RETIRED: JANUARY 1, 1997
STYLE # 4085
HANG TAG GENERATION: 4
ESTIMATED VALUE: $250–$300

Several Beanies share style numbers; Righty shares his with Bronty the brontosaurus. Another thing Righty shares is his poem, which appears on the tag of his fellow 1996 presidential election commemorative Beanie, Lefty the donkey. They're the only two Beanies of different styles that have the same poem. Political pundits may think Righty's flag should be on his right side, but that would put the flag's stars too close to his hind end—dishonoring the flag. Some of Righty's tags feature the "sufrace" misspelling. Rightys with an upside-down flag or no flag at all are considered very valuable.

Ringo
(the raccoon)

Ringo hides behind his mask
He will come out, if you should ask
He loves to chitter, He loves to chatter
Just about anything, it doesn't matter!

BIRTHDAY: JULY 14, 1995
DATE RELEASED: JANUARY 7, 1996
DATE RETIRED: (CURRENT)
STYLE # 4014
HANG TAG GENERATION: 3–5
ESTIMATED VALUE: $5–$7

Ringo's body style is similar to that of Sly the fox, Stinky the skunk, and Bucky the beaver, but his black eye mask and black-ringed tail help him stand out from the crowd. Although Ringo is cute, he is neither rare nor particularly hard to find, and his secondary-market value reflects these facts. Still a current, he is an affordable, and very lovable, addition to any collection.

Roary
(the lion)

Deep in the jungle they
crowned him king
But being brave is not
his thing
A cowardly lion some
may say
He hears his roar and
runs away!

BIRTHDAY: FEBRUARY 20, 1996
DATE RELEASED: MAY 11, 1997
DATE RETIRED: (CURRENT)
STYLE # 4069
HANG TAG GENERATION: 4–5
ESTIMATED VALUE: $5–$7

When Roary made his television debut on the *Today* show a few weeks before the official announcement of his release, he was still nameless. Nonetheless, his appearance sparked great excitement among Beanie collectors nationwide. His long, plush mane, which is similar to Nuts the squirrel's tail, is a delight to stroke. Because of the longer plush on the end of Roary's tail, the tail has a seam on the inside, unlike some of the other jungle cats, who have flat tails.

Rover
(the dog)

This dog is red and his
name is Rover
If you call him he is sure
to come over
He barks and plays with
all his might
But worry not, he won't
bite!

BIRTHDAY: MAY 30, 1996
DATE RELEASED: JUNE 15, 1996
DATE RETIRED: MAY 1, 1998
STYLE # 4101
HANG TAG GENERATION: 4–5
ESTIMATED VALUE: $12–$15

Red Rover, red Rover, let this Beanie come over! Rover bears a
strong resemblance to Clifford the Big Red Dog from the popular
series of children's books by Norman Bridwell and, for that reason,
is highly sought after by fans of the books. The resemblance had
also caused many to wonder if Rover would be retired early, but
Rover was available for two years before his May 1, 1998, retirement. Rover is also popular as part of the much-loved Beanie dog
group.

Scoop
(the pelican)

All day long he scoops
up fish
To fill his bill, is his wish
Diving fast and diving
low
Hoping those fish are
very slow!

BIRTHDAY: JULY 1, 1996
DATE RELEASED: JUNE 15, 1996
DATE RETIRED: (CURRENT)
STYLE # 4107
HANG TAG GENERATION: 4–5
ESTIMATED VALUE: $5–$7

Scoop hasn't been one of the more popular Beanies, but with the release of his Teenie Beanie "child" in the second McDonald's set, he'll become more difficult to find as people search for the original to go with their Teenies. Because of the new demand, his value on the secondary market is likely to increase. With his huge orange beak, Scoop is an unusual-looking Beanie—one that definitely stands out on a shelf full of currents!
Teenie Beanie (second set)

Scottie
(the Scottish Terrier)

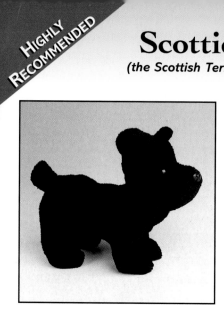

Scottie is a friendly sort
Even though his legs are short
He is always happy as can be
His best friends are you and me!

BIRTHDAY: JUNE 15, 1996
DATE RELEASED: JUNE 15, 1996
DATE RETIRED: MAY 1, 1998
STYLE # 4102
HANG TAG GENERATION: 4–5
ESTIMATED VALUE: $25–$30

Scottie is one of only two Beanie Babies to have two birthdays (Freckles is the other). You can find Scottie with a June 3, 1996, birthday as well as a June 15, 1996, birthday. While this is a point of minor interest, collectors should note that there is no additional value associated with either birthday. But if Scottie's hang tag also has the word "always" spelled "slways," that makes him more rare. Scottie is one of just five Beanies with napped fur rather than the standard smooth plush, and he's the only one with napped fur who is retired.

Seamore
(the seal)

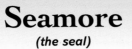

Seamore is a little white
seal
Fish and clams are her
favorite meal
Playing and laughing in
the sand
She's the happiest seal
in the land!

BIRTHDAY: DECEMBER 14, 1996
DATE RELEASED: JUNE 25, 1994
DATE RETIRED: OCTOBER 1, 1997
STYLE # 4029
HANG TAG GENERATION: 1–4
ESTIMATED VALUE: $125–$150

Collectors who found Seamore before her October 1, 1997, retirement, were very lucky indeed. She was extremely difficult to find for months before her retirement. As a result, her post-retirement value has skyrocketed well past that of the other Beanies in her retirement class. Finding Seamore in mint condition with clean white plush can be tricky, but collectors who don't already have this seal should get her now. Her price is sure to continue upwards.
Teenie Beanie (first set)

Seaweed
(the otter)

Seaweed is what she
likes to eat
It's supposed to be a
delicious treat
Have you tried a treat
from the water?
If you haven't, maybe
you "otter"!

BIRTHDAY: MARCH 19, 1996
DATE RELEASED: JANUARY 7, 1996
DATE RETIRED: (CURRENT)
STYLE # 4080
HANG TAG GENERATION: 3–5
ESTIMATED VALUE: $5–$7

Seaweed can either lie on her back or sit up straight. In her little otter paws she holds a piece of green felt seaweed (what else!). In this she is unusual, because she is the only Beanie to hold something in her hands. Many collectors expect her to join her pal Seamore in retirement soon. If you think so too, you "otter" add her to your collection. Her value may increase significantly due to her recent scarcity in stores.

Slither
(the snake)

(No poem)

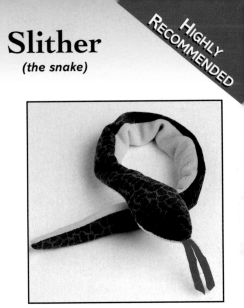

BIRTHDAY: (NONE)
DATE RELEASED: JUNE 25, 1994
DATE RETIRED: JUNE 15, 1995
STYLE # 4031
HANG TAG GENERATION: 1–3
ESTIMATED VALUE: $1,900–$2,100

This is one snake collectors need not fear. Slither's nearly two-foot length makes him the longest Beanie Baby there is. Finding Slither in any kind of decent condition is quite a feat, though, because his long, red felt tongue often takes the brunt of hard play, and his yellow underside is hard to keep clean. Either stretched out to his full length or coiled up and ready to strike, Slither is one of the most desired Beanies around.

Sly
(the fox)

Sly is a fox and
tricky is he
Please don't chase
him, let him be
If you want him just
say when
He'll peek out from
his den!

(brown belly)	**(white belly)**
BIRTHDAY: SEPTEMBER 12, 1996	BIRTHDAY: SEPTEMBER 12, 1996
DATE RELEASED: JUNE 15, 1996	DATE RELEASED: AUGUST 6, 1996
DATE RETIRED: AUGUST 6, 1996	DATE RETIRED: (CURRENT)
STYLE # 4115	STYLE # 4115
HANG TAG GENERATION: 4	HANG TAG GENERATION: 4–5
ESTIMATED VALUE: $175–$200	ESTIMATED VALUE: $5–$7

Sly sneaked onto the market with a brown belly at first release, but in keeping with its policy of trying to make Beanie physiology accurate, Ty soon replaced the brown-bellied version with a white-bellied one. The brown-bellied Sly can still be found at moderate prices, but this most likely won't be the case as collectors realize his rarity, especially if Sly is retired soon. It's a good idea for collectors to pick up one of each while there's still time.

Smoochy
(the frog)

Is he a frog or maybe a
prince?
This confusion makes
him wince
Find the answer, help
him with this
Be the one to give him a
kiss!

BIRTHDAY: OCTOBER 1, 1997
DATE RELEASED: DECEMBER 31, 1997
DATE RETIRED: (CURRENT)
STYLE # 4039
HANG TAG GENERATION: 5
ESTIMATED VALUE: $5–$7

For those who thought Legs the frog was too plain, Smoochy
should raise no complaints. He's modeled after a tree frog native to
Costa Rica and South America. You can tell his origins by his big,
bright toes and large eyes (which are red in real life). Tree frogs use
these unique features to aid their climbing. While Smoochy is a
fabulous addition to any Beanie collection, his status as a current
Beanie is reflected in his reasonably low secondary-market value.

Snip
(the Siamese cat)

Snip the cat is Siamese
She'll be your friend if
you please
So toss her a toy or a
piece of string
Playing with you is her
favorite thing!

BIRTHDAY: OCTOBER 22, 1996
DATE RELEASED: JANUARY 1, 1997
DATE RETIRED: (CURRENT)
STYLE # 4120
HANG TAG GENERATION: 4–5
ESTIMATED VALUE: $5–$7

In the feline world, the Siamese rule supreme . . . or so they think.
Snip, the Beanie Siamese, imparts this feeling of superiority with
her regal bearing and beautiful blue eyes. The darker spots on a
Siamese's nose, tail, and paws are called "points," and they come in
a variety of colors: chocolate, lilac, seal, and blue (which is actually
gray). Snip features tan plush with chocolate points, and she is a
welcome addition to the popular Beanie cat family.

Snort
(the bull)

**Although Snort is not so tall
He loves to play basketball
He is a star player in his dreams
Can you guess his favorite team?**

BIRTHDAY: MAY 15, 1995
DATE RELEASED: JANUARY 1, 1997
DATE RETIRED: (CURRENT)
STYLE # 4002
HANG TAG GENERATION: 4–5
ESTIMATED VALUE: $5–$7

When Tabasco the bull was retired, Snort was brought into the Beanie pasture as his replacement. The two Beanies are almost identical, except Snort's hooves (often referred to as "paws") are white instead of solid red like Tabasco's. In addition, the name is the only difference in their poems. Some Snorts were released in Canada in fall 1997 featuring Tabasco's poem, even though the name on the tag read Snort. This little red Beanie bull is popular with Chicago Bulls basketball fans as well as with Beanie collectors who want to pair him with Teenie Snort from the original McDonald's collection.
Teenie Beanie (first set)

Snowball
(the snowman)

There is a snowman, I've been told
That plays with Beanies out in the cold
What is better in a winter wonderland
Than a Beanie snowman in your hand!

BIRTHDAY: DECEMBER 22, 1996
DATE RELEASED: OCTOBER 1, 1997
DATE RETIRED: DECEMBER 31, 1997
STYLE # 4201
HANG TAG GENERATION: 4
ESTIMATED VALUE: $25–$35

Guaranteed not to melt in your hand, Snowball was released and retired quickly along with the 1997 Holiday Teddy. With a body similar to that of Spooky the ghost, who was also retired at that time, Snowball usually has a red scarf with white yarn fringe. But some scarf variations have been reported, including a counterfeit version with green string fringe! Snowball's value should increase dramatically, given his short period of availability. Many collectors never got the chance to see him in stores, but his current secondary-market value is still reasonable enough for most people to consider picking him up.

Sparky
(the Dalmatian)

Sparky rides proud on
the fire truck
Ringing the bell and
pushing his luck
He gets under foot when
trying to help
He often gets stepped
on and
Lets out a yelp!

BIRTHDAY: FEBRUARY 27, 1996
DATE RELEASED: JUNE 15, 1996
DATE RETIRED: MAY 11, 1997
STYLE # 4100
HANG TAG GENERATION: 4
ESTIMATED VALUE: $125–$150

Ever the helpful fire dog, Sparky let the cat (or should we say "dog"?) out of the bag in early spring 1997 when he was seen sporting "Dotty" tush tags. The rumors that there was a new dog on its way were confirmed when Sparky was retired—due to a trademark dispute with the National Fire Protection Association—and replaced with the almost-identical Dotty. (Sparky's ears and tail are white and spotted, while Dotty's are black.) Sparky is still fairly affordable if collectors want to add him to their Beanie kennel.

Speedy
(the turtle)

Speedy ran marathons in
the past
Such a shame, always
last
Now Speedy is a big star
After he bought a racing
car!

BIRTHDAY: AUGUST 14, 1994
DATE RELEASED: JUNE 25, 1994
DATE RETIRED: OCTOBER 1, 1997
STYLE # 4030
HANG TAG GENERATION: 1–4
ESTIMATED VALUE: $25–$35

Speedy, one of the smallest Beanie Babies, is only slightly larger than Trap the mouse. Speedy had been on the market quite a while when he was included as one of the Teenie Beanies in the original McDonald's set, prompting renewed interest in him as people ran to get matching Beanie "moms" for their Teenies. He's still quite affordable as a retired Beanie Baby, and his value has nowhere to go but up.
Teenie Beanie (first set)

Spike
(the rhinoceros)

Spike the rhino likes to
stampede
He's the bruiser that you
need
Gentle to birds on his
back and spike
You can be his friend if
you like!

BIRTHDAY: AUGUST 13, 1996
DATE RELEASED: JUNE 15, 1996
DATE RETIRED: (CURRENT)
STYLE # 4060
HANG TAG GENERATION: 4–5
ESTIMATED VALUE: $5–$7

Spike's disappearance from retailer shelves in late summer and fall 1997 led to rumors that placed him on the endangered Beanie list. Since then, he's been spotted more frequently. He's still quite popular. After two years on the current list, it may be about time for Spike's retirement. As a hard-to-find release, he'll probably do well on the secondary market; if you see him, herd him into your collection.

Spinner
(the spider)

Does this spider make
you scared?
Among many people that
feeling is shared
Remember spiders have
feelings too
In fact, this spider really
likes you!

BIRTHDAY: OCTOBER 28, 1996
DATE RELEASED: OCTOBER 1, 1997
DATE RETIRED: (CURRENT)
STYLE # 4026
HANG TAG GENERATION: 4–5
ESTIMATED VALUE: $5–$7

The Beanie Babies collection had been without a spider since Web's retirement in January 1996. Just in time for Halloween 1997, Spinner, with his beady red eyes and tiger-striped back, made his appearance. Speaking of his tiger-striped back, collectors will recognize it as the same plush used for the out-of-production "dark" Stripes the tiger. In spring 1998, Spinners started appearing in the United Kingdom with "Creepy" tush tags. Savvy collectors immediately snapped to attention, thinking this might be the sign of a future Beanie.

Splash
(the whale)

Splash loves to jump and
dive
He's the fastest whale
alive
He always wins the
100 yard dash
With a victory jump he'll
make a splash!

BIRTHDAY: JULY 8, 1993
DATE RELEASED: JANUARY 8, 1994
DATE RETIRED: MAY 11, 1997
STYLE # 4022
HANG TAG GENERATION: 1–4
ESTIMATED VALUE: $100–$125

The magnificent Splash, one of the original nine Beanie Babies, displays a striking contrast on his beautiful black-and-white belly. Look for an alternate poem on fourth-generation Splashes: "Maybe it's because she sprained a limb/But Splash never learned how to swim/I'm sure Splash is happy that you caught her/Just be careful not to leave her under water!" Still priced fairly reasonably, Splash is an excellent buy on the secondary market.

Spooky
(the ghost)

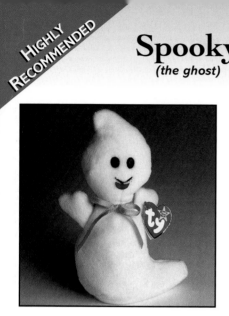

Ghosts can be a scary
sight
But don't let Spooky
bring you any fright
Because when you're
alone, you will see
The best friend that
Spooky can be!

BIRTHDAY: OCTOBER 31, 1995
DATE RELEASED: SEPTEMBER 1, 1995
DATE RETIRED: DECEMBER 31, 1997
STYLE # 4090
HANG TAG GENERATION: 3–4
ESTIMATED VALUE: $30–$35

A spooky thing happened on the way to Spooky's retirement. On January 29, 1997, Ty announced that Spooky and Radar the bat were retired. The company then turned around the next day and rescinded the announcement, sending collectors into a minor uproar. Spooky's mouth had several variations, but the most important error on this Halloween Beanie was a set of third-generation hang tags on which his name appeared as "Spook." Spooky is the only Beanie ever to have carried his designer's name, Jenna Boldebuck. This attribution is seen only on third-generation tags.

Spot
(the dog)

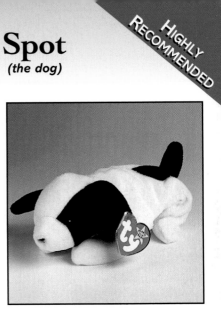

See Spot sprint, see
Spot run
You and Spot will have
lots of fun
Watch out now, because
he's not slow
Just stand back and
watch him go!

(without spot)	*(with spot)*
BIRTHDAY: JANUARY 3, 1993	BIRTHDAY: JANUARY 3, 1993
DATE RELEASED: JANUARY 8, 1994	DATE RELEASED: APRIL 13, 1994
DATE RETIRED: APRIL 13, 1994	DATE RETIRED: OCTOBER 1, 1997
STYLE # 4000	STYLE # 4000
HANG TAG GENERATION: 1–2	HANG TAG GENERATION: 2–4
ESTIMATED VALUE: $1,900–$2,100	ESTIMATED VALUE: $50–$60

Spot, one of the original nine Beanie Babies, was initially released without the spot on his back! This spotless Spot is very rare and is highly sought after by serious Beanie collectors. Those searching for the spotless dog should beware—there are counterfeits on the market. The more common, spotted version is quickly becoming scarce, and its value is increasing rapidly. Collectors who don't already own Spot should take him home while they still have the chance.

Spunky
(the Cocker Spaniel)

Bouncing around without
much grace
To jump on your lap and
lick your face
But watch him closely, he
has no fears
He'll run so fast, he'll
trip over his ears!

BIRTHDAY: JANUARY 14, 1997
DATE RELEASED: DECEMBER 31, 1997
DATE RETIRED: (CURRENT)
STYLE # 4184
HANG TAG GENERATION: 5
ESTIMATED VALUE: $5–$7

This cute little blond Cocker Spaniel was an instant hit when he arrived on the market. He was one of the first of his Beanie class to be plucked from the shelves. His big, floppy ears are covered with long, wavy plush that is different from all the other Beanie dogs. As part of the very popular dog group of Beanies, and certainly among the cutest, Spunky is a great addition to any collection.

Squealer
(the pig)

Squealer likes to joke around
He is known as class clown
Listen to his stories awhile
There is no doubt he will make you smile!

BIRTHDAY: APRIL 23, 1993
DATE RELEASED: JANUARY 8, 1994
DATE RETIRED: MAY 1, 1998
STYLE # 4005
HANG TAG GENERATION: 1–5
ESTIMATED VALUE: $25–$30

Anyone who thinks pigs can't fly should have seen these little piggies do just that as they flew off retailers shelves! Squealer enjoyed great popularity as a member of the original nine Beanie Babies. Just prior to his expected retirement announcement on May 1, 1998, Squealer became increasingly more difficult to find. Lucky collectors snapped him up before he was officially retired. His price as a retired may actually drop a bit for a short while before it takes off, so grab one if you can.

Steg
(the stegosaurus)

(No poem)

BIRTHDAY: (NONE)
DATE RELEASED: JUNE 3, 1995
DATE RETIRED: JUNE 15, 1996
STYLE # 4087
HANG TAG GENERATION: 3
ESTIMATED VALUE: $750–$900

Short and squat, Steg is tie-dyed in tones of yellow, tan, brown, green, and teal. Stegs with large spots of green and teal have proved to be the most popular. As is the case with all the tie-dyed Beanies, each Steg is unique in its pattern. Unlike his dinosaur mates, Bronty and Rex, who have a tendency to be a little bit limp, Steg is consistently round and plump. Though he has been the least popular of the three Beanie dinosaurs, Steg is still a very desirable and valuable member of the Beanie family.

Sting
(the stingray)

I'm a manta ray and my
name is Sting
I'm quite unusual and
this is the thing
Under the water I glide
like a bird
Have you ever seen
something so absurd?

BIRTHDAY: AUGUST 27, 1995
DATE RELEASED: JUNE 3, 1995
DATE RETIRED: JANUARY 1, 1997
STYLE # 4077
HANG TAG GENERATION: 3–4
ESTIMATED VALUE: $160–$190

As beautiful and graceful as a real-life stingray, Sting's beautiful
blue-and-green tie-dye reflects the colors of the ocean. Beware of
seam problems at the place where Sting's tail meets his body. If the
stitches are loose, his value could decrease considerably. Sting's
unique style and tie-dye patterns are irresistible. His price is
reasonable now, but it is likely to go up soon, so pick him up while
you can.

Stinky
(the skunk)

Deep in the woods he
lived in a cave
perfume and mints were
the gifts they gave
He showered every night
in the kitchen sink
Hoping one day he
wouldn't stink!

BIRTHDAY: FEBRUARY 13, 1995
DATE RELEASED: JUNE 3, 1995
DATE RETIRED: (CURRENT)
STYLE # 4017
HANG TAG GENERATION: 3–5
ESTIMATED VALUE: $5–$7

Stinky has a body style similar to that of Bucky the beaver, Ringo the raccoon, and Sly the fox, but he is distinguished by the broad white stripe down his back and tail. Confidence is high among the collecting community that this little stinker will retire soon, but there is still time to find him in stores before he's retired to the secondary market. Those who grab the black-and-white plush now will only be smelling the sweet smell of success when he is pulled from the shelves for good.

Stretch
(the ostrich)

She thinks when her
head is underground
The rest of her body
can't be found
The Beanie Babies think
it's absurd
To play hide and seek
with this bird!

BIRTHDAY: SEPTEMBER 21, 1997
DATE RELEASED: DECEMBER 31, 1997
DATE RETIRED: (CURRENT)
STYLE # 4182
HANG TAG GENERATION: 5
ESTIMATED VALUE: $5–$7

Modeled after Pinky the flamingo, Stretch turned out to be the
most difficult to find of the January 1998 class of Beanies. She has
long, tan legs and a white ring around her neck, and she has been
very well accepted by Beanie collectors due to her unusual shape.
As a current Beanie, Stretch doesn't command the high secondary-
market prices of some of the other, more rare Beanie Babies.

Stripes
(the tiger)

Stripes was never fierce
nor strong
So with tigers, he didn't
get along
Jungle life was hard
getting by
So he came to his
friends at Ty!

(dark, narrow stripes)	*(light, wide stripes)*
BIRTHDAY: JUNE 11, 1995	BIRTHDAY: JUNE 11, 1995
DATE RELEASED: JANUARY 7, 1996	DATE RELEASED: JUNE 3, 1996
DATE RETIRED: JUNE 3, 1996	DATE RETIRED: MAY 1, 1998
STYLE # 4065	STYLE # 4065
HANG TAG GENERATION: 3	HANG TAG GENERATION: 4–5
ESTIMATED VALUE: $275–$325	ESTIMATED VALUE: $12–$15

The original Stripes is known as "dark" Stripes. His gold color is darker than the newer Stripes, and his stripes are narrower and closer together. At the same time Stripes got fourth-generation tags, his coat was changed to a lighter gold, almost caramel, color, and his stripes were widened. To figure out which is which, try matching Stripes against Spinner the spider's back, which uses the same fabric as the dark tiger. A rare version of the dark Stripes has a more fuzzy plush sewn on his belly. This "fuzzy-belly" Stripes is the most valuable of the three. As a new retiree, the lighter Stripes is still a good buy.

Strut
(the rooster)

Listen closely to "cock-
a-doodle-doo"
What's the rooster
saying to you
Hurry, wake up sleepy
head
We have lots to do, get
out of bed!

BIRTHDAY: MARCH 8, 1996
DATE RELEASED: JULY 12, 1997
DATE RETIRED: (CURRENT)
STYLE # 4171
HANG TAG GENERATION: 4–5
ESTIMATED VALUE: $5–$7

When Ty encountered a potential trademark problem with Doodle the rooster, the company renamed him Strut and kept the same style number and poem. Because Strut wasn't redesigned in any way, owners won't know if they're looking at him or Doodle unless they check the tag. Tie-dyed in bright coral, yellow, hot pink, magenta, and sometimes green, Strut was used in a Beanie Baby promotion with the NBA's Indiana Pacers on April 2, 1997. He's still hard to find, but chances are he won't fly the Beanie coop for quite some time.

Tabasco
(the bull)

Although Tabasco is not
so tall
He loves to play
basketball
He is a star player in his
dreams
Can you guess his
favorite team?

BIRTHDAY: MAY 15, 1995
DATE RELEASED: JUNE 3, 1995
DATE RETIRED: JANUARY 1, 1997
STYLE # 4002
HANG TAG GENERATION: 3–4
ESTIMATED VALUE: $175–$225

Ty ran into yet another trademark problem with Tabasco, who was retired and quickly followed by his almost identical twin, Snort. Tabasco sports red hooves; Snort has white hooves. Tabasco's skyrocketing value on the secondary market is legendary, and collectors who had neglected to pick him up as a current release kicked themselves. Tabasco's rapid ascent has since slowed to match most of the rest of his retiring class, but he's still a great Beanie to own—especially for fans of the NBA's Chicago Bulls.

Tank
(the armadillo)

This armadillo lives in
the South
Shoving Tex-Mex in
his mouth
He sure loves it south
of the boarder [sic]
Keeping his friends in
good order!

(seven lines without shell)
BIRTHDAY: FEBRUARY 22, 1995
DATE RELEASED: JANUARY 7, 1995
DATE RETIRED: JANUARY 7, 1996
STYLE # 4031
HANG TAG GENERATION: 3
ESTIMATED VALUE: $175–$200

(nine lines without shell)
BIRTHDAY: FEBRUARY 22, 1995
DATE RELEASED: JUNE 3, 1995
DATE RETIRED: (UNKNOWN)
STYLE # 4031
HANG TAG GENERATION: 4
ESTIMATED VALUE: $175–$225

(with shell)
BIRTHDAY: FEBRUARY 22, 1995
DATE RELEASED: (UNKNOWN)
DATE RETIRED: OCTOBER 31, 1997
STYLE # 4031
HANG TAG GENERATION: 4
ESTIMATED VALUE: $65–$80

Tank started out life with seven lines of stitching and without the shell that gives armadillos their tanklike look. The second Tank had nine lines of stitching but still no shell. To appease collectors who protested the mistake, sometime during fall 1996 Ty finally outfitted Tank with a shell. The newest Tank was smaller and shorter, and his nose lacked the thread nostrils seen on the previous two Tanks.

Teddy
(the new-faced bear)

Teddy wanted to go out today
All of his friends went out to play
But he'd rather help whatever you do
After all, his best friend is you!

(brown only)

BIRTHDAY: NOVEMBER 28, 1995 (brown), (NONE) (cranberry, jade, magenta, teal, violet)

DATE RELEASED: JANUARY 7, 1995

DATE RETIRED: OCTOBER 1, 1997 (brown), JANUARY 7, 1996 (cranberry, jade, magenta, teal, violet)

STYLE # 4050 (brown), 4052 (cranberry), 4057 (jade), 4056 (magenta), 4051 (teal), 4055 (violet)

HANG TAG GENERATION: 2–4 (brown), 2–3 (cranberry, jade, magenta, teal, violet)

ESTIMATED VALUE: $75–$100 (brown), $1,850–$2,200 (cranberry, jade, magenta, teal, violet)

The new-faced bears can be distinguished easily from the old-faced bears because of their pouty look and the eyes placed inside the seams on their faces. The new-faced brown Teddy is the only one of the colored Teddys that wasn't retired in January 1996. He's also the only Teddy who has a poem. The new-faced bears tend to be more popular (and more expensive) than the more traditional old-faced bears, but owning any of the bears will make you the envy of other collectors. Violet seems to be the rarest and most popular of the new-faced version.

Teddy
(the old-faced bear)

(No poem)

BIRTHDAY: (NONE)
DATE RELEASED: JUNE 25, 1994
DATE RETIRED: JANUARY 7, 1995
STYLE # 4050 (brown), 4052 (cranberry), 4057 (jade), 4056 (magenta),
4051 (teal), 4055 (violet)
HANG TAG GENERATION: 1–2
ESTIMATED VALUE: $2,900–$3,250 (brown), $1,750–$2,000 (cranberry,
jade, magenta, teal, violet)

Teddy certainly has multiple personalities! These bears are among the most desired of the retired Beanies because of their beautiful colors and because they're bears — the most popular Beanie group. Of the old-faced bears, the brown is the most rare, even though he's the least rare of the new-faced bears. None of the old-faced bears has a ribbon around its neck, so don't worry if you see one without. (Actually, you should beware if you see one with a ribbon!) The old-faced bears have pointier noses and eyes set on the outside of the two seams that run from the ears to the nose. *(Not shown: brown old-faced teddy)*

Trap
(the mouse)

(No poem)

BIRTHDAY: (NONE)
DATE RELEASED: JUNE 25, 1994
DATE RETIRED: JUNE 15, 1995
STYLE # 4042
HANG TAG GENERATION: 1–3
ESTIMATED VALUE: $1,300–$1,500

Teeny, tiny Trap is the smallest of the Beanie family. His sleek, light-gray plush is accented by tiny pink feet, nose, ears, and tail, in addition to long, black string whiskers. Hopes are running high among collectors that Ty will introduce a replacement for Trap that is as cute as he is. If you can afford to overlook the retired value on Trap (which is enormous), this mouse is just too adorable to bypass.

Tuffy
(the terrier)

Taking off with a
thunderous blast
Tuffy rides his
motorcycle fast
The Beanies roll with
laughs & squeals
He never took off his
training wheels!

BIRTHDAY: OCTOBER 12, 1996
DATE RELEASED: MAY 11, 1997
DATE RETIRED: (CURRENT)
STYLE # 4108
HANG TAG GENERATION: 4–5
ESTIMATED VALUE: $5–$7

Given his terrier background, Tuffy was aptly named, since terriers are probably the most stubborn of the canine family. Tuffy is one of only five Beanies that have napped plush rather than the smooth plush seen in the vast majority of the Beanie collection. Collectors lucky enough to own an early-production Tuffy should check his hang tag to see if his name appears in all capital letters. The all-capital name gives him added value, so keep a leash on him if you have one!

Tusk
(the walrus)

Tusk brushes his teeth
everyday
To keep them shiny, it's
the only way
Teeth are special, so you
must try
So they will sparkle
when You say "Hi"!

BIRTHDAY: SEPTEMBER 18, 1995
DATE RELEASED: JANUARY 7, 1995
DATE RETIRED: JANUARY 1, 1997
STYLE # 4076
HANG TAG GENERATION: 3–4
ESTIMATED VALUE: $140–$175

Tusk can be found with a fourth-generation tag error that spells his name as "Tuck" instead of "Tusk." The "Tuck" version is more rare and, as such, is worth a little more on the secondary market. Don't worry about whether your Tusk's tusks face forward or backward—either is proper and doesn't affect his value one way or the other. Given his older retirement date, Tusk is still well within reach on the secondary market and is a good bet to increase in value in the future.

Twigs

(the giraffe)

Twigs has his head in
the clouds
He stands tall, he stands
proud
With legs so skinny they
wobble and shake
What an unusual friend
he will make!

BIRTHDAY: MAY 19, 1995
DATE RELEASED: JANUARY 7, 1996
DATE RETIRED: MAY 1, 1998
STYLE # 4068
HANG TAG GENERATION: 3–5
ESTIMATED VALUE: $12–$15

This plump giraffe with bright orange-and-yellow spots and tiny
horns is completely lovable. Many collectors correctly predicted
Twigs's May 1, 1998, retirement, and they busily tried to add him to
their collections before he disappeared from retailers' shelves.
Twigs's long-term value should be strong in the retired market,
especially because he is also now a "mom" to Teenie Twigs from the
second McDonald's Teenie Beanie set.
Teenie Beanie (second set)

Valentino
(the bear)

His heart is red and full
of love
He cares for you so give
him a hug
Keep him close when
feeling blue
Feel the love he has for
you!

BIRTHDAY: FEBRUARY 14, 1994
DATE RELEASED: JANUARY 7, 1995
DATE RETIRED: (CURRENT)
STYLE # 4058
HANG TAG GENERATION: 2–5
ESTIMATED VALUE: $5–$7

Valentino, a longtime favorite, has probably seen his last Valentine's Day as a current. He's been around for three February holidays already, fueling speculation that Ty will release a new Beanie in his place next year. Valentino with fifth-generation hang tags is the hardest to find, especially since these were among the tags that misspelled "origiinal" and "suface." This white bear resides in the Baseball Hall of Fame in Cooperstown, New York—a memento of the day David Wells of the New York Yankees pitched a perfect game. Valentino was given to fans as part of a Beanie promotion at Yankee Stadium that day.

Velvet

(the panther)

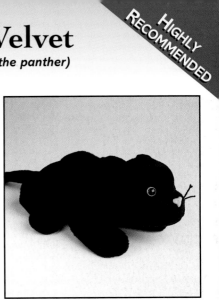

Velvet loves to sleep in the trees
Lulled to dreams by the buzz of the bees
She snoozes all day and plays all night
Running and jumping in the moonlight!

BIRTHDAY: DECEMBER 16, 1995
DATE RELEASED: JUNE 3, 1995
DATE RETIRED: OCTOBER 1, 1997
STYLE # 4064
HANG TAG GENERATION: 3–4
ESTIMATED VALUE: $25–$35

Velvet's pinky-peach nose is a striking contrast to the rest of her silky, all-black body. Although she's been retired since October 1997, Velvet was easy to find in stores just before her retirement, so she can still be found on the secondary market for a reasonable price. If you don't have her yet, get her while you can. She may become more difficult to find over time, and her price will reflect it.

Waddle
(the penguin)

Waddle the Penguin likes to dress up
Every night he wears his tux
When Waddle walks, it never fails
He always trips over his tails!

BIRTHDAY: DECEMBER 19, 1995
DATE RELEASED: JUNE 3, 1995
DATE RETIRED: MAY 1, 1998
STYLE # 4075
HANG TAG GENERATION: 3–5
ESTIMATED VALUE: $12–$15

Short and stout, this little penguin looks like he's wearing a tuxedo. Waddle is now finding favor with collectors because he is a "mom" to the Teenie Beanie Waddle, found in the second McDonald's promotion. Collectors also seek the well-dressed penguin because of his status as a new retiree. Due to the many collectors still searching for him, his value on the secondary market is likely to increase steadily.
Teenie Beanie (second set)

Waves

(the whale)

Join him today on the
Internet
Don't·be afraid to get
your feet wet
He taught all the Beanies
how to surf
Our web page is his
home turf!

BIRTHDAY: DECEMBER 8, 1996
DATE RELEASED: MAY 11, 1997
DATE RETIRED: MAY 1, 1998
STYLE # 4084
HANG TAG GENERATION: 4–5
ESTIMATED VALUE: $12–$15

Waves could never totally replace Splash, the original whale, but he makes a place of his own in Beanie history. He and Echo the dolphin were originally released wearing each other's tags, causing confusion among collectors. Eventually the tag mistake was rectified, and the mistagged versions of both Beanies are slightly more valuable than those with the correct tags—especially now that both are retired. Waves's relatively short life as a current should mean high secondary-market values for him as a retired.

Web
(the spider)

(No poem)

BIRTHDAY: (NONE)
DATE RELEASED: JUNE 25, 1994
DATE RETIRED: JANUARY 7, 1996
STYLE # 4041
HANG TAG GENERATION: 1–3
ESTIMATED VALUE: $1,400–$1,700

The Beanie Babies collection went almost two years without a spider after Web was retired and before Spinner was introduced. From the top, Web at first looks rather dull and unimaginative, with a black plush body, head, and legs, and little black eyes. But turn this arachnid over and you'll see a bright red stomach! Web's legs have a seam from tip to mid-leg. This seam makes his legs look jointed; when he is placed on his belly, his legs can be bent to look like he's ready to scamper away.